Team of the Century

Team of the Century
The Greatest High School Football Team in Texas

Al Pickett

State House
Press
McMurry University
Abilene, Texas

BIG COUNTRY ATHLETIC
HALL of FAME

The publication of this book is sponsored in part by the Texas State
Technical College (TSTC) West Texas Big Country Athletic Hall of
Fame. Because of the number of students and coaches from the Team
of the Century who have either been inducted or possibly will be
future inductees, it is fitting that the TSTC Big Country Athletic Hall
of Fame support this work.

Part of the proceeds from The Team of the Century will benefit two scholarship
funds honoring Chuck and Doris Moser. The scholarships are noted on page 172.

Library of Congress Cataloging-in-Publication Data

Pickett, Al.
      Team of the century : the greatest high school football team in
      Texas / Al Pickett.
      p. cm.
      ISBN 1-880510-87-1 (pbk. : alk. paper)
    1. Abilene High School (Abilene, Tex.)--Football--History. I. Title.
GV958.A35T43 2004
796.332'62'09764727--dc22

                              2004012447

State House Press
McMurry University, Box 637
Abilene, Texas 79697
(325) 793-4682
www.mcwhiney.org

Printed in the United States of America

1-880510-87-1
10 9 8 7 6 5 4 3 2 1

Book Designed by Rosenbohm Graphic Design

This book is dedicated to my father, Wayne Pickett, who first taught me the love of sports. He was my biggest supporter and a shining example of what a father should be. He was eager to read this book, having followed the research and writing. Unfortunately, he died in April before he had a chance to read the finished product. Not a day goes by that I don't think of him.

Contents

Foreword

We were seated in a West Texas coffee shop, reminiscing as we getting-old codgers are often wont to do these days. Our paths had crossed on the occasion of the funeral of Billie Ruth Loving, a wonderful and unforgettable Abilene High English teacher we shared during our teenage years. And Dr. Charles McCook—classmate, life-long friend, and one of the Chuck Moser quarterbacks you will read about in this fascinating history—was soon taking me on a sweet, nostalgic journey. Not only to Miss Loving's English class where her no-nonsense demands were exceeded only by her love of the language and her students, but to the playing fields of a time and place that only the maturation process can make one fully appreciate. It's one of the few really good things about reaching the age where you finally qualify for Senior Citizen discounts and Social Security.

Dr. McCook, like me and so many of our mutual high school buddies, is now a grandfather, no longer concerned over a receding hairline and the ever-present aches and pains that regularly visit a body finally growing a bit tired. His life and career accomplishments are a comforting primer of galloping success. Which is a point that can be made of so many who passed through the Abilene High athletic program, our teenage home away from home back when the '50s were fast rolling toward the '60s. I rarely miss the opportunity these days to brag that I have friends who are now doctors and lawyers, high dollar investment whizzes, coaches, teachers, and bankers—men who have made their marks.

"We were blessed," Charles says. Not by pampered wealth, blue-blood status or even particularly remarkable academic or athletic talent. Truth is, superstars were in short supply in our day despite the glowing tribute this book offers. The positive results—state championships, college scholarships, successful lives and careers—were part of a difficult-to-describe but very real collective effort. There were teachers like Miss Loving and coaches like the legendary Coach Moser, hard-working and hands-on involved parents, good neighbors and a community support I've not been witness to since taking leave of Abilene.

And, we agreed, there was a lasting mutual respect on the part of those who participated on those storied Eagles teams. It was more than Moser's magical winning streak, you know. Coach Blacky Blackburn's baseball teams also won their share of state championships, and Coach Bob Groseclose's track teams dominated their sport. Yet not everyone who earned his letter was selected to All-This or All-That teams, not all won gold medals or college scholarships or received big league bonuses. But each had his special place, an important role to play, his contribution judged as vital to victory as that of the teammate whose trophy case and scrapbook overflowed.

Pardon my venture into pop psychology, but it is my best guess that the insistence on such close and cooperative effort, everyone doing his share, however big or small, to the best of his ability put the real shine on the athletic program I was fortunate enough to have been a part of. Oh, we didn't go around spouting all that trite one-for-all, all-for-one b.s. But, truth be known, that was what it was about.

On the first day we reported for football two-a-days as sophomore students, there was nothing that hinted to me that my tall and skinny neighbor down the block, David Parks, would one day be named to any all-state team, or go on to become an all-American at Texas Tech or an all-pro with the San Francisco 49ers. He simply sweated through each painful practice with the rest of us, worked his tail off to get a little better every day, and judged defeating next week's opponent as the ultimate goal. I suppose he could have justifiably taken a bit of an aloof posture in later life, looking back at the days spent in our rag-tag company with some degree of bemusement. But he, like all others I've maintained friendships with for soon to be a half century, not only commanded respect but dished it out in ample dosage. That was just the way, then. And now.

It was a few years ago at an impromptu reunion organized by Stuart Peake, yet another AHS grad-turned-doctor, when Parks stood, looking over the large gathering. Every coach of our generation was still alive and present on that day. And so were many of those who had played for them. "Some of these guys," Parks said, "I haven't seen in years. But it is just like we talked yesterday. There was such a closeness back then. And it's still there. Always will be."

That, then, is what this book is about. A tightly-bound brotherhood in a simpler time and place when everything came together to produce something quite special. You had to have been there.

Carlton Stowers
Abilene High School, Class of '60

Introduction

Friday the thirteenth is supposed to mean bad luck. But a Friday the thirteenth more than fifty years ago may have been one of the more fortunate days in the history of Abilene, Texas. That was the day—February 13, 1953—that the Abilene Independent School District hired a young thirty-four-year-old coach named Chuck Moser to be the new head football coach at Abilene High School.

Moser's hiring made the front page of the local paper the next morning, but it was not the lead story. That spot belonged to an economic story about declining livestock prices that were costing the nation's ranchers billions of dollars.

On the sports pages were stories about Abilene Christian College's 55-47 victory over cross-town rival McMurry College in basketball and the Abilene Eagles' 64-56 road basketball victory over Odessa. Sports editor Dick Tarpley was in Fort Worth to cover Golden Gloves boxing, a popular sport in Abilene at the time.

"The Stooge," starring Dean Martin and Jerry Lewis, was playing at the stylish Paramount Theatre in downtown Abilene. The Paramount was also featuring a midnight show, "Niagara," starring Marilyn Monroe. Grissom's, a local department store, was offering the "Skirt of the Year" for $10.95, a great gift idea for "your valentine."

Nothing could match the lasting impact on a community that Moser's hiring had on Abilene.

The school board meeting story the next day in the *Abilene Reporter-News* contained no comments from Superintendent A.E. "Poly" Wells or any of the board members as to why they chose Moser. The story in the paper said only that the board met for three

Members of the Abilene board of education that hired Chuck Moser were Ollie McMinn, Bert Chapman, Mrs. T.E. Roberts, W.E. Fraley (president), Mrs. George Swinney (secretary), Roy Skaggs and Morgan Jones Jr. (vice president)

and a half hours, narrowing a list of twenty-one names considered for the position down to six.

According to the February 14 edition of the *Reporter-News*, other names considered by the board included some famous coaches, like Gordon Wood of Stamford, who eventually became the state's winningest high school football coach and captured nine state championships at Stamford and Brownwood. The list of potential coaches included John Tomlin of Port Arthur, John Whinnery of Dumas, Ty Bain of Kilgore, Gene Corrotta of Tulsa Central, Owen Erekson of Brenham, Jay Fikes of Littlefield, Guy Gardner of Borger, Bill Hinton of San Angelo, Mike Murphy of Stephenville, Marion Priddy of Gainesville, Theo Rigsby of Alice, Pete Roach of Mineral Wells, Al Johnson of New Mexico Western College, Johnnie Kitchen of Austin, Gene McCallum of Port Neches, Al Milch of Sul Ross College, Moon Mullins of Anson, Bill Sheffield of Lufkin, and Elmer Simmons, an assistant coach at the University of Houston.

After narrowing its list down to an unnamed six finalists, the board then voted unanimously to offer the job to Moser. The Abilene board's decision would be a stroke of genius. Moser's hiring proved to be a marriage made in heaven between the soft-spoken disciplinarian and a community that loved its high school football. What followed were seven of the most amazing years in the rich history of Texas high school football.

The Eagles won three consecutive state championships, captured six straight district titles in a rugged league known as "The Little Southwest Conference" and fashioned the nation's longest winning streak at the time, forty-nine victories in a row under Moser's tutelage. Moser compiled an amazing 78-7-2 record during his seven-year coaching tenure in Abilene. The three consecutive state championships have been equaled only three times in the state's largest classification—by Waco in 1925-27, Amarillo in 1934-36, and Midland Lee in 1998-2000.

The records established by Moser's Eagles remain the standard by which high school football teams all over the state of Texas are judged. So remarkable was that era of Abilene football that the *Dallas Morning News* in 1999 named the Eagles of 1954-57 the Texas High School Football Team of the Century. Suddenly, an era revered in Abilene as the Glory Years or the Moser Years was receiving statewide recognition again, nearly a half-century after Abilene's "Warbirds" were the dominant force in Texas high school football.

What made Moser so successful? Why did a team that had won only one district title since the end of World War II suddenly become such a juggernaut? Why is Moser still remembered so fondly by his former players, fifty years after they played for him and nearly a decade after his death? What made a seemingly otherwise ordinary group of high school kids become the best high school football team in Texas history? How did Moser work his magic to galvanize an entire community in support of his program? What are the lessons taught by Moser that are still applicable to today's athletes?

Those are questions that I have often asked during my eighteen years in Abilene as I heard the stories about Moser's remarkable success in the 1950s, and those are the questions I hope to answer in a book whose time has come. The fall of 2004 marks the fiftieth anniversary of the first of Abilene's three consecutive state championships.

My thanks to many of Moser's former coaches and players who gave their support to this project. Also, a special thanks to Dick Tarpley, the long-time *Reporter-News* editor who kept a remarkable file of clippings and pictures on the Moser Years, and to AISD-TV's Rob Westman, who provided a videotape of a 1988 interview with Moser. Lynn Nichols, a former Abilene High assistant principal, helped me obtain pictures and other memorabilia from the museum he maintains at the school, and Abilene High principal Terry Bull and his secretary Paula Tallant went out of their way to provide help on this project.

My hope is this book will preserve for all time the story of the greatest high school football team in Texas history, The Team of the Century.

Al Pickett

CHAPTER 1

A Reluctant Applicant

Jimmy Millerman looked like the All-American boy with his blond hair. His 5-foot-11 inch frame carried 157 pounds as a sophomore in 1952. By the time he was a senior all-state running back, he had filled out to 185 pounds. He was not only a running back on the high school football team in Abilene, Texas, but also a star sprinter on the Eagles' track team.

Bobby Jack Oliver, a year older than Millerman, was a strapping 6-3, 225-pound lineman, the largest player on the Abilene High School football team.

Abilene Superintendent A.E. "Poly" Wells was looking for a new football coach when he decided to seek the advice of the Eagles' two returning starters.

"He called us into his office, which was located in Abilene High School (now Lincoln Middle School) back then," Millerman said.

"It looks to me we have two choices," Wells said to Millerman and Oliver. "We can go with an older guy who has a proven track record, or we can go with a young guy who has a fresh approach and has a good record." Wells mentioned former Southern Methodist University coach Rusty Russell as a possible "older" coach who was interested in the job.

Millerman said he's not sure why, but both he and Oliver told Wells they would rather have a younger coach.

"Mr. Wells came to us and asked us our opinion of another coach," Oliver recalled. "Then he asked what type of coach we want-

Chuck Moser compiled a 78-7-2 record in seven seasons at Abilene High

ed—a younger coach or an older, more experienced coach. We didn't know what to say. We finally said a younger coach."

Wells invited the younger coach— Chuck Moser, a thirty-four-year-old native of Missouri who had just nine years of head coaching experience, including seven at McAllen in the Rio Grande Valley—to interview for the job.

When Moser came to Abilene for his interview, Wells called on Millerman and Oliver again. "I remember he came and got us out of class," Millerman said. "He said he'd like to have us meet a prospective new coach, or words to that affect. He invited us in to talk to him. We had never heard of Chuck Moser."

But the new coach certainly made a quick impression on the pair. "He was very intense," Oliver said, "and he had those eyes that could look through you. You knew he was in charge."

How much the two players' recommendation influenced Wells' decision is probably lost to eternity, but Wells recommended Moser to the Abilene school board, which voted to hire him. It was a decision that changed the history of high school football in Abilene and had a profound influence on hundreds of lives. It brought together a community in support of a high school football team.

More than fifty years later, Moser's Abilene Eagles are still remembered as the Texas high school football "Team of the Century."

PETE SHOTWELL

The greatest era in Texas high school football almost didn't happen, however. In fact, it wouldn't have if it hadn't been for Moser's last-minute change of mind.

Abilene superintendent A.E. 'Poly' Wells is credited with selecting Chuck Moser to be the Eagles' head football coach in 1953.

Abilene was looking for a replacement for Prince Elmer "Pete" Shotwell, a coach who was a legend in his own right, when Wells sought Moser. Shotwell, for whom Abilene's current 15,000-seat football stadium is named, was in his second stint as the coach at Abilene High School. But on February 1, 1953, he was named the supervisor of health and physical education for the Abilene Independent School District, a move Shotwell apparently had requested. He held that position for several years before moving to McMurry College, where he served as the school's athletic director from 1957-67.

Shotwell, who never had a losing season in thirty-six years as a head coach, is still the only Texas high school football coach to win state championships at three different schools. He came to Abilene in 1919 after coaching one year at Cisco and serving a year in World War I following his graduation from West Texas State. He enjoyed immediate success, leading the Eagles to four district titles in five years. The Warbirds reached the state semifinals in 1920 and 1921 before losing to Waco in the 1922 finals. Abilene finally won a state championship in 1923 with a 3-0 victory over Waco. The state championship was the first for both Shotwell and Abilene, although both would win two more before Shotwell's retirement from coaching in 1953. No one, however, could have envisioned the success that his successor would enjoy.

Shotwell left Abilene High the first time after the 1923 season. He coached two years at Hardin-Simmons University and one year at

Sul Ross College in Alpine before returning to the high school ranks in 1927 at Breckenridge. The Buckaroos battled Port Arthur to a 0-0 tie in the 1929 title game, giving Shotwell his second state championship, albeit a co-championship. In 1935, he moved on to Longview, where he claimed his third state championship in 1937.

Abilene, meanwhile, won state championships in 1928 and 1931 under Dewey Mayhew, the school's all-time winningest coach.

Shotwell returned to Abilene in 1946. He had success, compiling a 43-26-3 record in seven seasons and winning a district championship in 1949. But the Eagles tallied three consecutive 6-4 seasons before Shotwell stepped down following the 1952 campaign.

NEW DIRECTION

"The B-team was undefeated in 1952, but, no, I don't think anyone dreamed what would happen," said Twyman Ash, who, like Millerman, was a sophomore on Shotwell's final team in 1952. "We wouldn't have gotten there without Moser. Shotwell was a great guy and a great coach, but things had gotten to a stagnant state. He saved every scrap of rubber. We had game helmets and practice helmets. We had an old Camp Barkeley field house at Fair Park. When Moser came in, he threw everything away. Shotwell was a real penny pincher. The first change we noticed was when Moser started buying all new equipment. Moser ordered us black and white uniforms, just like Lubbock. He said 'We may never beat Lubbock (the 1952 Class AAAA state champion), but we'll look like them.'"

"He was a master psychologist," Oliver said of Moser. "He came in and had me try on one of those new uniforms. They were slick black pants and a shiny white jersey with a black stripe. I thought I was three or four inches taller in that uniform."

Millerman had great respect for both Shotwell and Moser. "Both were great coaches," he said. "Of course, I was under Moser for a lot more games. But Shotwell was a great motivator, too. He could fix those dark eyes on you and say you need to do it this way. And you knew that was the way you needed to do it."

Moser had led McAllen to the state semifinals in 1952. But when Wells went looking for Shotwell's replacement, Moser was no longer at McAllen; he had just taken a new job at Corpus Christi Miller.

"I had moved to Corpus Christi and taken the job at Corpus Christi High School," Moser recalled in a 1988 interview. "After I had been there for three days, bought a house and moved in, Mr. Wells called and asked me to interview for this job. I wasn't very interested. I said let me talk to my wife. She said, 'You better go up there because every time you get beat you're going to wish you had.' So I flew up there two days later and talked to Mr. Wells.

"He was real smart. After we talked, he got Bobby Jack Oliver, who was a 225-pound tackle—just a great-looking kid—and Jim Millerman, who was a real fast runner, to show me around the school. I had heard of both of them. I wasn't looking much at the school. I was looking at Jim and Bobby Jack most of the time. I'm not sure if that isn't why I'm here."

Hardin-Simmons University coach Murray Evans, who played for a couple of years in the National Football League, may have also had a hand in Moser's hiring. Evans coached at Kingsville in 1950 before returning to HSU as an assistant under Warren Woodson. His Kingsville team played Moser's McAllen squad that year.

"Moser was my best friend and the best football coach I ever saw, other than maybe Warren Woodson," said Evans, interviewed shortly before his death. "He knew a lot about football and he didn't mind getting on the kids. He's as good as I ever witnessed."

Wells' persistence obviously paid off because Moser accepted the job in Abilene. The Abilene school board chose Moser from among twenty-one candidates, offering him the head coaching job and a $7,000 annual salary on Friday, February 13. Moser started his new job on March 1, 1953, less than a month after moving to Corpus Christi to take another "new" job. Moser and his wife Doris had two daughters, Janie, age seven, and Glenn, age two, when he came to Abilene. He had compiled a 63-22-2 record in nine previous seasons as a head coach.

SCHOLAR-ATHLETE

Born September 9, 1918, at Chillicothe, Missouri, Moser played football, basketball, and baseball there and became an all-conference center on Don Faurot's University of Missouri team that went to the Sugar Bowl in 1939. Moser began his coaching career in Lexington, Missouri. After two years, he joined the Army Air Corps, became a navigator at Kelly Air Base in San Antonio, and met his future wife, a student at the University of Texas. Chuck and Doris married October 25, 1942, while he was stationed at Hondo.

Moser was a bright student in addition to being an outstanding athlete—named a top scholar-athlete three times at Missouri and selected the top scholar in athletics in the Big Six Conference as a senior. That emphasis on academics would be a hallmark of Moser's coaching career.

His hiring in Abilene in 1953 proved to be the right coach at the right place at the right time.

CHAPTER 2

The Staff

"For one thing, I had a terrific staff," Moser said years later when asked for the secret of the Eagles' success during his tenure in Abilene. "Hank Watkins was a good friend of mine. He was the head coach at Donna when I was at McAllen. He used to come over to my office every Sunday afternoon and we'd talk.

"When I took this job, the first thing I did was call Hank. He's as good a line coach as ever coached the line. No question about it. I always said give me a good quarterback and a great line coach and

Brainstorming sessions by head coach Chuck Moser (with pencil) and assistants (left to right) Wally Bullington, Shorty Lawson, Blacky Blackburn and Bob Groseclose helped direct the Eagles' 49-game winning streak from 1954-57. (Photo courtesy of Abilene High museum)

you can win some ballgames. Bear Bryant tried to hire him (at Texas A&M after Watkins coached at Abilene High) but instead he went to Houston. He could coach for anybody."

Indeed, it was a remarkable staff that included Watkins, Bob Groseclose, Shorty Lawson, B.L. "Blacky" Blackburn, Nat Gleaton, and Wally Bullington. In fact, each is a member of at least one Hall of Fame or received significant recognition for various achievements.

Watkins was the only assistant Moser brought with him when he came to Abilene. He retained Groseclose, Lawson, and Blackburn from Shotwell's staff and then hired Gleaton away from Coleman to be the Eagles' basketball coach. An unusual set of circumstances led to the addition of Bullington to Moser's staff.

HANK WATKINS

Watkins spent four years (1953-56) in Abilene as Moser's line coach and top assistant. During that time frame, the Abilene Eagles won forty-six of the fifty-one games they played.

What made the Eagles so successful?

Hank Watkins

"Chuck Moser," Watkins said. "I have a lot of respect for him as a person and as a coach. We worked well together. I can't say enough good things about Chuck. Kids just wanted to play for him."

Watkins, who had played college football at Tulane, was coaching at Class AA Donna, while Moser was at nearby McAllen. When Moser took the job at Corpus Christi Miller, he hired Watkins to join him.

"That's where I'd gone to high school," Watkins said.

But a few days later, Moser changed his mind and decided to take the Abilene job. Moser's loyalty helped Watkins secure a job in Abilene. "I didn't have a job if he didn't stay at Corpus Christi,"

Watkins said. "When Chuck met with Poly Wells, he told him he couldn't take the Abilene job if I didn't come, too. It was a step up to go from a 2A school to first assistant at a 4A school."

Watkins spent Friday nights on the headphones in the press box. "The day before the game, Chuck and I would meet," he said. "He wanted to make sure we were on the same page. We'd check it out before the game. In the heat of the game, if I'd call something down to him, he'd never second-guess me.

"We were doing things that other teams weren't doing, like an off-season program. We worked them out so they'd be able to build their bodies. By the time they were juniors and seniors, they were all in such great condition, not only big and quick but strong. We had a run of kids that wanted to play good. I was very fortunate. Chuck was such a good leader."

Watkins coached some outstanding linemen at Abilene, like all-staters Stuart Peake and Sam Caudle. "Those were two of my favorites," he said. "But we had a lot of good linemen. Jimmy Rose was a great center, and Elmo Cure was a pretty good stud. Rufus and Boyd King were outstanding linemen. Freddie Green was a great punter, and Bobby Jack Oliver was the biggest lineman we had the whole time I was there." Watkins said Oliver could "cave in the whole side of the line."

"I used him for a demonstration on how to ward off a block by getting up under your opponent's shoulder pads," he said, chuckling. "I told him to fire out and hit me. He said, 'Coach, do you really want me to do that?' Well, he did, and the first thing that hit was the back of my head on the ground. I remember everyone snickering."

Bear Bryant tried to hire Watkins at Texas A&M following the 1956 season, but Watkins turned him down. "I told him I appreciated the offer," Watkins said. "You know how Bear was. He just said you've got your reasons, and I've got mine. But we remained good friends. I'm probably one of the few guys to ever turn down Bear Bryant."

Instead, Watkins took a job coaching the linebackers and ends at the University of Houston. "I hated college coaching," he said. "You had to be gone so much and recruit and lie and try to butter up the kids you were recruiting. In three years, I never spent a Thanksgiving Day with my family."

Watkins left Houston after three years and returned to high school coaching, spending eight years as the head coach at McAllen. He then retired from coaching and spent the next twenty years working in the textbook business.

BOB GROSECLOSE

Groseclose was the Eagles' track coach. He was a native of Breckenridge and had played for Shotwell with the Buckaroos. He coached Abilene High to four state track championships before leav-

Bob Groseclose

ing in 1960 to take over the University of Louisiana-Monroe track program.

Groseclose, a member of the ULM and Louisiana Sports Halls of Fame, led then-Northeast Louisiana University to nineteen conference championships while producing fourteen individual national champions and world record holders in six events, including John Pennel, the first person to break seventeen feet in the pole vault. He coached the Indians from 1960 through 1989. The tracks at both Abilene High and Louisiana-Monroe are named in honor of Groseclose.

B.L. 'BLACKY' BLACKBURN

Blackburn, who also grew up in Breckenridge, played for Shotwell and later coached with him at Longview. Shotwell hired Blackburn away from Fort Stockton in 1947 to coach baseball, which had just become a University Interscholastic League sport. Blackburn had never coached baseball until his first season in Abilene in 1948.

He compiled a record of 409 wins and 205 losses in twenty-five seasons (1948-72) in Abilene. Blackburn's Eagles won fourteen district championships, including nine in a row at one point. They advanced to the state tournament five times, making the championship game in four. The Warbirds lost a 2-1 heartbreaker to Paris in

the 1955 title game but won back-to-back state championships in 1956 and 1957, with many of the same players who helped the Abilene High football team win three consecutive state championships.

"Blacky Blackburn was one of the best baseball coaches ever," Moser said. "Seems like we went to the baseball playoffs every year. In fact, I had to have to spring practice in February, because in May most of our football

B.L. 'Blacky' Blackburn

players were still in baseball in the playoffs. Our track men would go to the state meet. So I'd have spring practice before we got so into track and baseball. It worked out good that way, except when it snowed."

Many credit Blackburn's efforts as the junior varsity coach and scout as keys to the Eagles' football success. Blackburn, also a noted math teacher, was inducted into the Texas High School Coaches Association Hall of Honor in 1973. Moser was selected to the THSCA Hall of Honor in 1968. Both Moser and Blackburn are members of the Big Country Athletic Hall of Fame. Abilene High's baseball stadium is named Blackburn Field. Blackburn died in June 2004.

NAT GLEATON

Gleaton, who flew B-17's over Germany in World War II, returned after the war to finish his degree at Howard Payne and was then hired as the basketball coach and football line coach at Coleman. Moser hired Gleaton to replace Jake Bentley as head basketball coach. The school board fired Bentley for an off-color comment he made to his team during the 1952-53 season, forcing Moser to look for a basketball coach almost immediately after arriving in Abilene.

"I didn't know Chuck, but Shorty Lawson and people like that recommended me," said Gleaton. "They needed someone to scout football on Friday nights. Chuck called and said, 'I understand you're a good basketball coach.'"

Nat Gleaton

Gleaton had won three district championships in four seasons at Coleman and had taken the Bluecats to the state tournament one year. Moser said he also wanted him to coach the sophomore line in football. Gleaton accepted the job in Abilene at a salary of $4,000 a year.

Not only did Gleaton play a part in the Eagles' amazing football success but he also enjoyed a great deal of success of his own in basketball.

Gleaton's basketball teams won two district titles in thirteen seasons, despite not having the football players available until Christmas because of the Eagles' lengthy postseason runs in football. His last basketball team in 1966 won the district championship and lost by one point in the second round of the playoffs to a Lubbock High team coached by future Texas Tech basketball coach and athletic director Gerald Myers.

Gleaton resigned in 1966 to go into the insurance business, a job he held for the remainder of his working career.

"I loved coaching," Gleaton said. "I taught American history and Western Civilization, and I loved that, too. But I couldn't make a living at it. I was making $8,500 that last year at Abilene High."

Gleaton and Groseclose would scout together one Friday night, while Bullington and Blackburn scouted together the next. Typically, if coaches scouted one week, they would be on the sidelines for the next game against that opponent.

"We'd come back on Friday night and put our scouting report together," Gleaton said. "Then Sunday at 2 P.M. we (the coaches) would be in the gym. Chuck wanted to go over the scouting report. He was thorough, and you'd better do it right. Everything was so coordinated. Quite frankly, he was the best I've been around. The players worshiped him. He had a way with kids."

SHORTY LAWSON

Lawson, who later followed Moser as the athletic director for the Abilene ISD, made his name as a football and basketball referee. He became a well-known major college official, working both sports in the Southwest Conference.

"I love sports, and I love officiating, and I love the people involved in it," Lawson said when he was inducted into the National High School Sports Hall of Fame in 1993. "I met the greatest people in all the world through officiating. It's a thrill to meet the people."

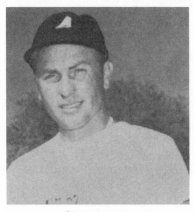

Shorty Lawson

Lawson, a native of Old Hickory, Tennessee, who first came to Abilene to attend Abilene Christian College in 1944, said the Texas-Arkansas football game in Fayetteville in 1969 was the highlight of his officiating career. The game, billed as the Big Shootout, matched the top-ranked Longhorns against number two-rated Arkansas. "That was the Game of the Century when President Nixon was there," he said. Lawson made a controversial call on the Razorbacks' first scoring drive, ruling an Arkansas receiver was in bounds at the two yard line. The Hogs took a 14-0 lead, but Texas rallied for a 15-14 victory to claim the national championship.

In his career, Lawson officiated three Cotton Bowl games, one Sugar Bowl, one Orange Bowl, one Liberty Bowl, two Fiesta Bowls, and two Sun Bowls. He also officiated four NCAA Division II bowl games and one NAIA bowl game.

Lawson worked twelve NCAA regional tournaments and thirteen NAIA national tournaments as a college basketball official. He retired from basketball officiating in 1975 after twenty seasons in the Southwest Conference and fifteen in the Missouri Valley Conference. His final game as a football official was in 1979.

In 1981, Lawson was inducted into the THSCA Hall of Honor, joining former colleagues Shotwell, Moser, and Blackburn.

Oddly enough, it was Lawson's basketball officiating career that led to Wally Bullington joining Moser's staff.

WALLY BULLINGTON

Bullington, a native of Athens, Alabama, had been an all-American center at Abilene Christian College in 1952 and was finishing up his degree in the spring of 1953 when he received the opportunity to work with Moser.

Wally Bullington

"Chuck was short of coaches because they were going to have early spring practice so as not to conflict with baseball and track," Bullington said. "He called Garvin Beauchamp (the ACC head football coach at the time) and asked if he had any seniors that would like to come over and work with the team during spring practice. Beach asked me and Ted Sitton (who also later became a head coach at ACU) to go over to Abilene High and work with Chuck."

Bullington had signed a contract to be an assistant coach at Weatherford that next fall, but, like Moser, changed his mind when the opportunity came to coach in Abilene. Moser called him after graduation early that summer and asked if he would come to Abilene

High as an assistant in football and basketball. Bullington accepted the job and never left Abilene.

"I think he really wanted Shorty (Lawson) to be the assistant in basketball, but Shorty couldn't because of his officiating. I often told Shorty if he hadn't been officiating basketball, I'd never gotten the job at Abilene High.

"It was the greatest training period I could have had as a young coach, working with Chuck. He was one of the best coaches I've ever known, and that includes all of them—high school, college, and the pros. He was way ahead of his time. He was very intense. He was very fundamentally sound. He really stressed fundamentals. He was a great motivator. He was the kind of guy you wanted to do your best for. He could get the best out of players. That was the secret to our success. He had the touch to get on a kid, and they'd still like him. I couldn't have had a better mentor."

Bullington was named Moser's successor following the 1959 season, leading the Eagles to a 40-19-1 record in the next six seasons.

"Chuck gave me the option of replacing him at Abilene High or taking the job at Cooper, the new high school," Bullington said. "But I was an Eagle by that time."

Bullington admitted that it was intimidating to follow the legendary Moser as the head coach at Abilene High. "I remember worrying about what if he shows up to practice," he said. "But the only time he was there was when I asked him to come. He made it a point not to be seen too much. That's how big a man he was. I felt he wanted me to do well."

Moser noted later that he hired only two guys directly out of college to be on the varsity staff during his career as a coach and athletic director. They were two pretty good ones, however—Bullington and David McWilliams, who later became the head coach at Texas Tech and the University of Texas.

Bullington left Abilene High after the 1965 season to become head coach at his alma mater. In nine years (1968-76) as the head football coach at ACU, his teams had a 62-32-2 record. Four of his nine teams were nationally ranked, and Bullington coached ACU to its first NAIA Division I national championship in 1973. He coached six first team all-America players, including all-pro running back Wilbert Montgomery.

Bullington also served as the athletic director at ACU from 1969 until his retirement in 1988, presiding over the Wildcats' transition from NAIA to NCAA Division II. He was inducted into the ACU Sports Hall of Fame in 1993.

HAROLD BRINSON

Harold Brinson replaced Hank Watkins as the line coach in 1957 when Watkins left to become an assistant coach at the University of Houston.

Brinson later earned his doctorate and became superintendent of the Abilene school district and then president of Southern Arkansas University. Long-time Abilene businessman Tommy Morris and Melvin Lindsey also served briefly on Moser's staff.

JUNIOR HIGH

H.P. Hawkins, the quarterback of Abilene's 1954 team, said a lot of credit should also go to Shotwell and the outstanding junior high coaches he hired, like Neal McClesky, Milton Bryant, and Gilbert McClesky.

"Pete Shotwell started the success in Abilene when he put in the elementary school program," Hawkins said. "Shotwell set the program in motion, putting good people in the junior highs. Boy, did that help. We had such good coaching. They were all quality men and set good examples. They were good teachers."

BEV BALL

The unofficial member of Moser's staff was Bev Ball. Moser hired the Throckmorton native to be the cheerleader sponsor, Bold Gold sponsor, and girls' tennis coach.

Ball made sure the cheerleaders and spirit squads played a key role in the Eagles' football success. "We had everything going for us,"

Moser said. "Our senior girls every year would try to outdo the senior girls from the year before as far as spirit."

Moser asked Ball to come over to AHS after one year at South Junior High. She wasn't much older than the Abilene High students when she first joined Moser's staff, but Ball spent the next forty-eight years at Abilene High, including fifteen as the tennis coach and thirty-two as the swimming coach for both Abilene High and Cooper.

"I was just one of the guys," said Ball, who calls Moser her "hero and mentor."

She was named the first recipient of the Abilene Rotary Club's Moser Coach of the Year Award in 1999. That same year, Ball retired from the Abilene ISD and became swimming coach at McMurry University. In 2003, she was inducted into the Big Country Athletic Hall of Fame, joining her former fellow coaches Moser and Blackburn.

Abilene High coaches were (front row, left to right) Wally Bullington, Chuck Moser, Hank Watkins, Bob Groseclose, (back row, left to right), Shorty Lawson, Tommy Morris, Blacky Blackburn and Nat Gleaton. (Photo courtesy of Flashlight)

CHAPTER 3

1953: A New Beginning

Although he began his new job on March 1, the Chuck Moser era officially began on September 1, 1953, the first day of two-a-day practices for the new Abilene High football coach.

Abilene was a growing city of nearly 60,000 by 1953. Billed as the Key City (the key to West Texas), Abilene is located 180 miles west of Dallas, on what is now Interstate 20. The city had battled back from the closure of Camp Barkeley, an Army base located just southwest of the city, at the end of World War II. The closing, it was feared, would turn Abilene into a ghost town, but in 1953 the city was in the process of becoming a military town again with the procurement of what would eventually become known as Dyess Air Force Base. Plans for the new Abilene base had been announced a year earlier. The week of September 1, 1953, marked the on-air debut of KRBC, Abilene's first television station.

Abilene had one all-white high school in 1953. The school system had not yet been integrated, so the city's African-American students attended Woodson High School, which also fielded a strong football team that competed in the state's Prairie View Interscholastic League, also known as the Negro League.

All three of Abilene's colleges had competitive football teams. Abilene Christian had won a small college national championship just two years earlier, and the Wildcats' schedule included a victory over Florida State in 1953.

Hardin-Simmons was playing in the powerful Border Conference that included Texas Tech, Texas Western (now Texas El-Paso), New Mexico State, Arizona and Arizona State. The Cowboys' non-conference schedule included Rice, Tulsa, and LSU in 1953.

McMurry was playing in the Texas Conference along with ACC, although Abilene Christian announced that year that it was leaving the conference to play a stronger, independent schedule.

Some of the great names in the three colleges' football history were coaching in 1953—Garvin Beauchamp at ACC, Murray Evans at Hardin-Simmons, and Wilford Moore at McMurry.

But, make no mistake about it, Abilene was a high school football town and the Abilene Eagles drew top billing. With that in mind, Abilene fans were eager to see their new coach in action. Frankly, expectations weren't that high. Even the local paper wrote that "the inexperienced Eagles are given no better chance to finish fourth in the strong 1-AAAA district."

Abilene Reporter-News sports editor Jack Holden picked the Eagles to finish fifth in the far-flung eight-team district. Holden picked Abilene behind Lubbock, Pampa, Amarillo, and Odessa, but ahead of San Angelo, Midland, and Borger is his preseason prediction.

A DIFFERENT APPROACH

The Eagles faced neighboring Stamford, a Class AA school, in a preseason scrimmage. The Bulldogs were coached by Gordon Wood, who eventually won 396 games and nine state championships— including two at Stamford—during his amazing career.

Stamford had also played Abilene in a preseason scrimmage a year earlier—Shotwell's final season—and Wood was critical of the Eagles in his autobiography, *Coach of the Century*:

"Seven days before our season opener, I loaded the team onto a school bus and drove them over to Abilene to scrimmage the Abilene High Eagles. My kids were scared to death. Abilene High School was ten times the size of Stamford. Abilene's coach was Pete Shotwell. He had two assistants, Shorty Lawson and Bob

Groseclose, who were capable coaches and knew what they were doing. His other three assistants were more of a hindrance than help. Instead of showing the Eagles' players what they were doing wrong and helping them, they made fun of the boys. Their whole attitude really bothered me. Coaches should be there to teach and help players improve. Young men respond to positive instruction. Ridicule seldom yields results."

A year later, Stamford faced Abilene again in a 1953 preseason scrimmage. This time, Wood noted a major change in the Eagles: "In August, near the end of our fall football camp, we scrimmaged Abilene High School again. The Eagles had a new head coach, imported from McAllen, Texas. The difference in coaching techniques was absolutely amazing. Every time an Abilene player made a mistake, an assistant coach was right there pointing it out, explaining what the boy had done wrong, patting him on the back and encouraging the young man to do better. The Eagles didn't look real sharp that afternoon, but I was confident Abilene's football fortunes would improve after the new coach got his message across."

Wood's feelings were prophetic. The *Dallas Morning News* named Wood the "Coach of the Century" in 1999, the same time that it selected Abilene as the "Team of the Century." Wood had high praise for Moser.

"We only scrimmaged him that one time," said Wood, who died at age eighty-nine after he was interviewed for this book, "but I learned a lot. He turned Abilene High from nothing to a great team in a hurry. Chuck was a great football coach, a strong, tough disciplinarian."

SEASON OPENER

Moser had just nine days to prepare his Eagles for their season opener against Dallas Highland Park, a traditional powerhouse that had produced the legendary backfield duo of Bobby Layne and Doak Walker just a decade earlier.

The Eagles were considered underdogs to Highland Park in their season opener at Fair Park Stadium, the city's football stadium at

South Seventh and Barrow Streets across from Rose Park. Today, Big Country Youth Football League players gain their initial football experience at Curly Hays Field on the same site where the powerful Eagles of the 1950s once soared.

Jimmy Millerman returns a punt 59 yards against Highland Park in 1953 for the first touchdown of the Chuck Moser Era at Abilene High

Abilene showed quickly in its season opener that this was a new era with Moser at the helm. Millerman scored on a fifty-nine-yard punt return and Wendell Phillips had a forty-two-yard touchdown run in the first quarter as the Eagles rolled over the Scots 28-13. The "Moser Era" was officially under way, and what an era it would be.

The Eagles followed up their surprisingly easy win over Highland Park with a 13-13 tie against Sweetwater. Millerman's eight-yard run for a touchdown on fourth down with just thirty-five seconds remaining—and H.P. Hawkins' extra-point kick—gave the Eagles a tie with a strong Mustang team.

A win and a tie may have been an impressive start to the new season, but the Eagles were again underdogs for game three. Abilene had to travel to Breckenridge to face the Buckaroos, two-time defending state champs who had not lost a game since the 1952 season opener against Wichita Falls. Breckenridge was ranked number one in the state in Class AAA, and heralded passer Kenneth Ford — who would go on to a stellar career at Hardin-Simmons—was the star quarterback for the highly touted Bucks.

The Eagles, however, were welcoming the return of all-state lineman Oliver—the player who had so impressed Moser on his initial visit to Abilene. Oliver had missed the first two games with a sepa-

Wendell Phillips and Bobby Jack Oliver's blocking paves the way for Don Harber's keeper for a touchdown against Breckenridge in 1953. (Photo courtesy of Flashlight)

rated shoulder. The underdog Abilene team rolled over the Buckaroos, 19-6, handing Coach Joe Kerbel just his second loss since arriving at Breckenridge a year earlier.

The Eagles' defense held the Bucks to only ninety-eight yards rushing and put heavy pressure on Ford. The Breckenridge quarterback was just seven of nineteen passing for ninety-six yards. Abilene quarterback Don Harber scored on a six-yard bootleg with just two seconds left before halftime.

"We outsmarted them," Millerman said of the Eagles' win over Breckenridge. "I had scored on a reverse against Sweetwater a week earlier. We were in almost the exact situation, and we ran the reverse again, only Harber faked to me and kept it on a bootleg. He just walked into the end zone untouched."

Millerman called the win over Breckenridge a critical victory in the development of Moser's program at Abilene. "I remember thinking after we won the game that if we can beat Breckenridge, there's no telling what we can do. I know they were a classification smaller than us, but they were the big guys because they had won so many state championships. I remember watching them beat Temple (in 1951 and '52) for the state championship at Fair Park Stadium in Abilene."

Fullback Hal McGlothlin (who later helped build Fairway Oaks Country Club in Abilene as a partner in the LaJet Corporation) and sophomore Henry Colwell scored on short runs in the second half to seal the Eagles' victory.

That same day, Cal Erskine struck out fourteen as the Brooklyn Dodgers beat the New York Yankees 3-2 in game three of the World Series. It was Brooklyn's only win of the Series, however, as days later the powerful Yankees completed a 4-1 Series win over their subway rivals.

The Eagles, now 2-0-1, were ready to open district play.

DISTRICT GAMES

Abilene began district play on October 9 with 60-0 romp over Borger. McGlothlin and Ronnie McDearman scored two touchdowns each.

"We had to do pushups on Mondays for every point we gave up (in the previous game)," said starting end Hollis Swafford. "We were doing calisthenics one day at practice, and Moser asked Jack Self what was wrong. He said, 'I feel sorry for Borger. They have to do sixty pushups.' He thought that was just part of football and every team had to do it."

Moser's love for "junk" plays was becoming evident. As the Eagles prepared for their next game against Odessa, the local paper noted that Moser had put in three special plays in the first four games and all three had worked for touchdowns. Moser told the paper he had put in five new plays for the Odessa game.

A standing-room-only crowd of 12,000 jammed Fair Park Stadium for the showdown with Odessa. The Eagles led all the way until the fourth quarter when quarterback Carl Schlemeyer—who completed thirteen of nineteen passes for 234 yards—rallied the Bronchos to a come-from-behind 19-14 victory. Millerman and Phillips scored first-quarter touchdowns to give Abilene a 14-0 advantage, but the Eagles couldn't contain Schlemeyer and hold the lead.

Millerman said a bad call cost Abilene the game—and possibly the district title. "I still remember the official's name—Burns

McKinney. He ruled interference on one of our defensive backs, and that led to the winning touchdown for Odessa."

The victory helped propel Odessa to the district championship, the last time in the 1950s that the district bell, given annually to the district football champion, would reside anywhere other than Abilene. Odessa advanced all the way to the state finals that year before losing to Houston Lamar.

The Eagles next lost a heartbreaker to Pampa. Harber's thirty-seven-yard bootleg late in the second quarter had given Abilene a 6-0 lead, but Oliver missed the extra-point kick. Fifteen seconds before halftime, the Harvesters scored on a 35-yard pass play, and Bob Wilhelm kicked the extra point to give Pampa a 7-6 lead. That was the final score as neither team could find the end zone in the second half on a cold night in the Texas Panhandle.

Abilene was now 3-2-1, having lost two in a row. It was a situation the Eagles would never again experience in the Moser era. In fact, Moser's teams would never again lose more than one regular-season game over the next six years.

The Eagles wouldn't lose again in 1953, either.

IMPRESSIVE ENDING

Abilene caught fire after its back-to-back losses to Odessa and Pampa. The Eagles outscored their opponents, 160-20, over the final four weeks of the 1953 season. The impressive streak began with a 32-7 romp over traditional power Amarillo.

Jack Holden wrote: "Statistically, it was one of the worst defeats in Amarillo history as the Warbirds rolled up 487 yards on the ground and through the air to a pitiful 91 by the Sandies." Moser used twelve different backs in the game, and junior quarterback H.P. Hawkins threw a pair of TD passes to Bob Gay for thirty-five and forty-eight yards.

After a week off, Abilene blanked defending state champion Lubbock, 28-0, at Texas Tech's Jones Stadium. The victory was Abilene's first over Lubbock since 1947 and marked only the second time the Westerners had been shut out under Coach Pat Pattison. Abilene rolled up 334 yards on the ground, led by Millerman, McGlothlin, McDearman and Phillips.

Wally Bullington called that victory over Lubbock a boost to the Eagles' confidence. "It proved we could play with anyone."

The Eagles continued their domination of opponents with a 39-13 win over Midland. Abilene scored six of the eight times it had the football, while guards Dick Orsini, John Thomas, and Frank Liles led the Warbirds' defense.

Moser's first season concluded with the traditional Thanksgiving Day game against San Angelo, a 61-0 humiliation of the Bobcats. Holder commented on the lopsided victory in the *Reporter-News*: "Moser sent everything but the pep squad into the game, 37 men listed on the Warbird roster seeing service. It didn't make any difference. The reserves scored just as often as did the first-stringers."

Abilene, picked to finish fifth in the district, concluded the season with a 7-2-1 mark and a second-place finish in District 1-AAAA. Only a tie with Sweetwater, a fourth-quarter rally by Odessa aided by a questionable pass interference call, and a heartbreaking one-point loss at Pampa prevented the surprising Eagles from going unbeaten in Moser's inaugural season.

"We felt good about our year," said Bobby Jack Oliver, who became the first all-stater under Moser. "It's always a disappointment if you don't win district, but we did OK. I hope we set the tone for the years that followed."

Plenty of victories would follow over the next six years, but the Eagles would no longer be called surprising. Abilene had officially arrived as a Class AAAA powerhouse in Texas high school football.

CHAPTER 4

Eligibility Slips

Moser's philosophy about the role of his football team in the school may surprise some.

"There is only one reason to have a good athletic program, and that's so you'll have a lot better school system," he said in an interview years after his coaching career had ended. "I got into my players and our athletic program that the best student in that class—maybe not the smartest—is the one who will set the example for listening and studying and passing those tests. If you do anything in that class that the teacher doesn't like, she will tell me and I will take care of it. The kids knew that. Our kids were smart, and they set good examples. In turn, the teachers loved us. We had some teachers who wanted to win worse than I did, if that's possible."

Moser's eligibility slips were as much a part of being an Eagle as going to practice itself. When Texas House Bill 72 passed in the mid-1980s, some observers considered the no-pass, no-play rule a revolutionary idea. It wasn't; Moser had his own form of no-pass, no-play fifty years ago. He required every player on his team to take an eligibility slip to each teacher each week. The teacher had to sign the slip, fill out the student-athlete's grade, attendance record, and attitude. The teacher could also make comments on the eligibility slip, which the student-athlete had to turn in to Moser each Monday. If a player wasn't passing three courses, he couldn't play the following Friday. That rule was set in stone and would later play a role in Abilene's winning streak.

SCHOLARSHIP ELIGIBILITY REPORT

Abilene High School

NAME_____ DATE_____

Every student who represents Abilene High School should be a representative student, passing at least three subjects since the beginning of the Semester.

Subject_____

Grade_____

Attendance_____

Attitude_____

Comments_____

Teacher_____

Signature_____

P .E. or Study Hall_____

TO THE STUDENT: On the day designated, present this slip to each teacher as you attend his or her class. Turn it in to your coach or sponsor at the end of the day.

TO THE TEACHER: Please indicate: (1) grade as passing or failing for the semester, (2) attendance as regular or irregular, (3) attitude as good, fair, poor.

NOTE: PLEASE USE INK

Chuck Moser required every player to get an eligibility slip signed by each teacher every week. (from Abilene High School Football Organization book)

"We require each boy to get his instructors to fill in this report each week during the entire school year," Moser said in a book that he published in 1959. The book, entitled *Abilene High School Football Organization,* was sold to coaches at clinics, where Moser was a frequent speaker.

"In 1959, he had me put together a book that summarized his program," assistant coach Wally Bullington said. "He'd had so many requests for information at clinics. We sold hundreds of them at coaching school that year. It sold for $2.50. It showed how he organized practice and drills, communication, bulletin board material, and eligibility slips. He had eligibility slips long before House Bill 72."

"We feel that in this way we can counsel with the boy in regard to his school work and encourage him to work harder in subjects where he is weak," Moser said in his book. "It also lets the boy know how he stands in his courses from the first of the grading period."

Twyman Ash, an all-state end on the Eagles' 1954 state championship team, said the eligibility slips were taken seriously. "If there
was any comment on it like you were talking too much in class, he
made you run. There was an old horse-racing track around the field
at Fair Park. It was five-eighths of a mile, and he sent you out there.
It was like running on a plowed field. Those teachers loved that guy."

David Bourland, starting quarterback on the Eagles' 1955 state
championship team, also learned the importance of the eligibility
slips. "The only time I ever got in trouble was my senior year. My
home room teacher, Mrs. Turner, wrote on the slip that I talked too
much. Coach Moser called me in. He said there's a comment on your
slip that you talk too much. He said, 'That's just ten hundred-yard
dashes after practice, but you can handle it.'" Bourland said Moser
made it clear to him that it better not happen again—and it didn't.

Bullington said Moser's version of no-pass, no-play had the support of teachers and parents. "The most important question on the
eligibility slip was attitude. The teachers loved it. It spilled over to the
whole school. They set the tone for attitude and discipline for the
whole school. And you'd better not try to forge a signature.

"The parents supported him. He'd tell the parents in a meeting
before the season started that he didn't know if their boys hung up
their clothes at home but they better not have any equipment lying
on the floor in the locker room. He was teaching them things for life.

"He had a curfew. He called enough to let them know he would
call. He wanted kids to do well in school, behave, be a role model,
and have a spiritual life. He taught a Sunday school class at St. Paul
Methodist Church."

The players took the curfew seriously. Hollis Swafford, a starting
end on Moser's 1953 and 1954 teams, said, "If you had a date on a
weekend and you were running late, you felt like he was at the door
waiting on you."

Moser's influence cast a long shadow over all of Abilene, from the
classroom to the playing field to his players' social life.

CHAPTER 5

1954: Discipline Pays Off

In 1954, Roger Bannister became the first runner to break the four-minute barrier in the mile. The Cleveland Indians set a major league record with 110 victories but lost to the New York Giants in the World Series, best remembered for Willie Mays' miraculous over-the-shoulder catch of Vic Wertz's deep drive to center field. During the first week of football practice, legendary football coach Pop Warner died at age eighty-three.

Slugger Joe Bauman, playing for a minor league baseball team in Roswell, N.M., hit his seventy-second home run, a professional single-season record that lasted until Barry Bonds of the San Francisco Giants belted seventy-three homers in 2001. New Texas A&M football coach Paul "Bear" Bryant took 111 players to a grueling preseason training camp in Junction but came home with only thirty-five, an event that became part of Aggie lore and has since been immortalized in a book and made-for-TV movie, *The Junction Boys*. On August 8, a new magazine called *Sports Illustrated* made its debut with Milwaukee Braves slugger Eddie Mathews on the cover.

In Abilene, the focus was on the upcoming high school football season. The Abilene Eagles, riding the wave of their strong finish in 1953 and returning a large number of players, were the preseason number one pick in Class AAAA. Abilene hadn't won a state football championship since 1931, but the state's sportswriters had made the Eagles the favorite to win the title in 1954.

1954 state champions

Prior to the start of workouts, quarterback H.P. Hawkins attended the practice sessions for the Texas High School Coaches Association's annual all-star game in August in Dallas. "That was back when college coaches coached the two all-star teams," Hawkins said. "Bobby Dodd (the legendary Georgia Tech coach) was coaching one of the two teams. I don't remember whether it was the South or the North. He was running the same offense that we were, so Coach Moser had suggested I go down there. I spent four or five days down there at my family's expenses. It helped me because Bobby Dodd was a great teacher. But so was Coach Moser.

"A lot of my teammates came down to watch the game. I remember as we were leaving, I turned back to see the Cotton Bowl sign on the side of the stadium and I said to the other guys, 'We'll be back here to play in the state championship game.' "

Hawkins' prediction would come true, sort of. The Eagles would appear in the state championship game later that year; but it wouldn't be in the Cotton Bowl.

TWO PLAYERS SKIP OUT

Only a couple of days into two-a-day practices, however, Abilene's attention was diverted to a problem. On Friday, September 3, end

Bob Gay and fullback Ronnie McDearman, both returning starters, went to the morning practice but didn't show up that night for the evening practice. Reports were the pair had made an "unexplained and unexpected trip" to California.

Jack Holden wrote in the local paper: "There's been much talk around Abilene this week concerning the disappearance of Bob Gay and Ronnie McDearman from the Eagle football squad. It's even caused considerable stir outside the city, enough that some quarters are dropping the Warbirds from the favorite's seat for the state AAAA crown. Biggest question now is whether Coach Chuck Moser will let the boys return to the squad if they return. That's his decision, of course, but it's doubtful."

David Bourland, a junior defensive back and backup quarterback on the 1954 team, said Gay and McDearman asked to rejoin the team when they returned from California.

"We used to have skull practice under the stands at Fair Park on Mondays," Bourland said. "Moser said, 'Ronnie and Bob have come back from California and want to be back on the team. I want to be fair, so we'll vote on it. But I vote no.' "

"You could hear a pin drop," said Bourland. Moser then raised his voice and said, "The reason I vote no is because nobody quits me."

Bourland said the team never actually voted on the return of Gay and McDearman. The players knew there was no need for a vote; Moser had made his decision.

Assistant Coach Wally Bullington said the decision to not allow the two players back on the team proved to be an important moment in the development of Moser's program. "They knew he meant business, and his rules were there for a reason," Bullington said. "He didn't write the kids off as people, though. Gay came back and was an outstanding trackman. He coached for a long time. He learned a valuable lesson."

Jimmy Millerman said the team members didn't necessarily think about the impact of Moser's rules. They just knew they had to step up and fill the void of the two missing players. "We thought, OK, two of our best players aren't here, so we better get it together," he said. "We knew it was going to be tough to lose two guys like that, but we can still do it."

Sam Caudle didn't really think much about the loss of Gay and McDearman, either. He knew Moser wouldn't let them back on the team when they returned from California. "We already knew what Moser said was the way it was going to be," Caudle said. "They left during two-a-days. At the time, I was so tired I really didn't think much about it. I was just trying to make another day."

OFF TO A FAST START

Millerman, Twyman Ash, and lineman John Thomas were elected team captains prior to the first game. Putting the controversy of Gay and McDearman behind them, the Warbirds opened the season like a number one ranked team. Abilene High scored in every quarter in a 40-0 rout of Dallas Highland Park. The Eagles followed that with a 13-0 blanking of Sweetwater. Millerman scored on a two-yard run, and Caudle and Ash pounced on a fumble at the Mustangs' twenty-seven-yard line in the third quarter to set up a two-yard scoring run by Henry Colwell.

Abilene was soaring with two shutout victories in two games. But waiting for the Eagles in week three was Breckenridge, the top-rated team in Class AAA. It was a much-anticipated number one vs. number one match-up at Fair Park Stadium.

Breckenridge ran a triple-option "belly" offense in which the quarterback would either hand off to the fullback or pull the ball back at the last moment. If he pulled it out, the quarterback had the option to run or pitch the ball to the trailing halfback. The Buckaroos' triple-threat attack of quarterback Bennett Watts and running backs Jakie Sandefer, Dick Carpenter, and Clyde Harris totally befuddled the Abilene defense. It was a talented group. Watts, Sandefer, and Carpenter went on to play for Bud Wilkinson at the University of Oklahoma, while Harris became an all-conference player at East Texas State.

Breckenridge whipped an Abilene defense that had posted two straight shutouts, beating the Eagles 35-13. Holden summarized the outcome in the next morning's Abilene paper:

"It was an unbeatable offense which the green-shirted Buckies threw at Abilene, a perfectly timed touchdown machine which gouged and bored and shoved the Eagles all over the sod at Fair Park Stadium."

Fifty years later, Abilene's Ash remembers the loss to Breckenridge like it was yesterday. "I was playing cornerback, and they were running a double option. They killed us. I'd come up and hit the fullback, and the halfback would go around me.

"The next Monday, I was dreading practice. I thought I'd probably lost my starting job. Coach Moser called us in and said, 'I want to apologize. I didn't have you prepared for what they were running. That won't happen again.' We were really well prepared after that."

Sophomore Stuart Peake was playing defensive end in front of Ash. "It didn't take Watts and Sandefer long to find the weak link," Peake said. "That was the only game I ever lost in high school."

The Eagles had to take the practice field on that Monday coming off a loss the previous Friday. That would not happen again for more than four years.

"Our attitude changed after that game," Thomas said. "The Breckenridge game was the turning point."

A Moser-coached team never again had a problem with an opponent running the triple-option "belly" offense, either.

"Jakie Sandefer killed us with the option pitch," Bullington said. "After that game, Chuck came up with a defense to stop the belly option. We assigned different people to responsibilities. One would take the quarterback, one would take the fullback, and one would take the pitch-man. It was designed to string the quarterback out and make the sideline our best tackler."

Peake, who eventually became an all-state and all-American guard and defensive end, said he learned to defend the option. "You don't have to be a big end. You have to be big enough to stop the off-tackle play and quick enough to beat the quarterback. You just have to look the quarterback in the eye and make him commit." Peake weighed 185 pounds and was actually one of the fastest players on the Abilene team. He ran a 9.8 in the 100-yard dash and ran on the Eagles' sprint relay team in track.

DISTRICT GAMES

Abilene bounced back from the loss to Breckenridge in a big way, opening district play with a 34-7 victory over Borger. H.P. Hawkins threw three touchdown passes, a twenty-yarder to Millerman and strikes of ten and forty-six yards to Colwell.

Next up was a trip to Odessa. The defending district champion Bronchos' late rally a year earlier had prevented Abilene from winning the district title. The Eagles turned the tables on Odessa this time with a 21-7 victory in front of 20,000 fans at Broncho Stadium, including 600 Abilene fans who made the trip to Odessa on the "Eagle Special" train.

The big play was a fifty-yard touchdown pass from Hawkins to Millerman with fifty-six seconds to go before halftime. Millerman, who scored the first touchdown of the game on a ten-yard run, polished off the Bronchos when he hauled in an eighty-five-yard TD pass from Hawkins later in the third quarter.

"Personally, that was probably my best game," Millerman said. "I scored all three touchdowns, and H.P. hit me down the middle for eighty-five yards. That was fun."

Hawkins, who said it was bedlam with the standing-room-only crowd in Odessa, noted out that the pass play to Millerman had just been put in that week, especially for the Odessa game.

"Odessa ran a defense that left the middle open about fifteen yards deep if we did certain things," he said. "Their adjustment left the middle open. They punted to us, and we had the ball on our own fifteen. As I went into the game, Coach Moser told me to call that pass play that we put in that week. Then Odessa called a time out. I had a lot of time to worry about the risk of throwing a pass that deep in our end of the field."

Did he ever consider changing the call?

"I didn't like the risk," said Hawkins, laughing, "but no way would I question Coach Moser."

The play worked to perfection. Odessa adjusted like Moser expected, and Hawkins hit Millerman for an eighty-five-yard touchdown.

Abilene, which lost only twice in 1953, avenged its other setback the following week with a 41-7 thrashing of Pampa at Fair Park Stadium. It was an impressive showing on both sides of the football for the Eagles.

The Abilene defense held the Harvesters' Harold Lewis to forty-three yards rushing, and the Eagles' offense rolled up 506 yards of total offense, including 380 on the ground. Millerman had 104 yards rushing and scored three touchdowns, while Colwell scored on a sixty-three-yard punt return.

Abilene fans also received a glimpse into the future. Sophomore Glynn Gregory, filling in for Glen Belew who had broken his arm a week earlier, had a forty-six-yard return of an intercepted pass to set up a touchdown and then scored himself on a seventy-six-yard run in the fourth quarter. Another sophomore, Jimmy Carpenter, scored the final touchdown on a thirty-one-yard punt return.

The names of Gregory and Carpenter would become legendary in Abilene over the next two years, but seniors like Hawkins, Ash, Millerman, and Colwell were the leaders of the 1954 Eagles, who seemed to be gaining momentum each week.

Abilene continued to roll, thrashing Amarillo 47-0 in the Sandies' worst-ever loss at home. Nine different Eagle backs gained a total of 389 yards rushing. Hawkins also completed three of four passes for ninety-seven yards and a pair of touchdowns, including a thirty-two-yarder to Swafford.

Abilene's domination on both sides of the football continued as October turned to November. The Eagles held Lubbock to only four net rushing yards in a 35-7 victory over the Westerners.

Fullback Jim Briggs had a career-best ninety-seven yards rushing against Lubbock. It would be his career-best for only one week, however.

MIDLAND GAME

The next week Abilene played at Midland in a game to decide the District 1-AAAA title. An estimated 1,600 fans made the trip from Abilene, including 850 who went by train on the "Eagle Special."

Ash remembers the game against Midland as a prime example of Moser's genius. "Midland had Wahoo McDaniel and they had a good team. Moser said we're going to have to hold Wahoo below 150 yards and our fullback, Jim Briggs, will have to rush for more than 150 yards. We go out there, and it was a helluva game. Wahoo was like a huge animal. I'd grab on to him and hang on until someone else got there to help bring him down."

But Moser's statements about Briggs outgaining McDaniel proved accurate as the Eagles beat Midland, 28-14, to claim Abilene's first district title under the new alignment.

Holden wrote in the *Reporter-News*: "Abilene's courageous Eagles didn't stop the Bulldogs' great Wahoo McDaniel Friday night, but they saw their own fullback, Jim Briggs, lead them to the city's first district championship by a 28-14 score. Briggs was magnificent as he tore up the purple line for 149 yards and outgained McDaniel by 20 yards."

McDaniel, still considered one of the greatest players in the history of the "Little Southwest Conference" went on to become an all-American at Oklahoma, played for the New York Jets, and then made quite a name for himself as a professional wrestler.

"I remember Wahoo coming through the line giving a war whoop," defensive tackle Rufus King recalled. "He'd start hollering the minute he got the ball. Coach Moser used to take all the school papers, and Wahoo was the sports editor of Midland's school paper. We used to read it and laugh because Wahoo would write about himself—'Wahoo did this and Wahoo did that.' "

McDaniel was the first back to really give the Eagles' defense problems since the loss to Breckenridge, but on this night he was outplayed by Abilene's undersized fullback. Briggs scored the first touchdown just three minutes into the game. Late in the first quarter, Bourland intercepted a pass and ran it back seventy-three yards for a score.

Bourland said the ball went right through McDaniel's hands and into his.

"I only weighed 142 pounds as a senior," Bourland said. "I tackled Wahoo thirteen times unassisted. Years later, Wahoo came into Abilene for a pro wrestling match, and called me up."

Wahoo remembered the pass that Bourland intercepted. "The ball hit my hands," he told Bourland. "When I got back to the bench, I never got such a butt-chewing in all my life."

The Eagles made it 21-0 when Millerman swept right end from four yards out with less than two minutes remaining before halftime. Abilene made the lead stand up in the second half. Hawkins scored the final touchdown on a one-yard keeper.

The buzz after the game was the tremendous power running of McDaniel, but it was Briggs who shined the brightest in the Eagles' T-formation offense. Moser told the Abilene paper after the game that his fullback plays were working so well he didn't dare switch off them. He used halfbacks Millerman and Colwell—the team's usual offensive stars—only sparingly.

With the district title already wrapped up, the Eagles closed out the regular season with a 27-0 whitewash of San Angelo. Millerman scored on a twenty-eight-yard reverse and a twenty-four-yard run, and Colwell added a one-yard TD plunge as Abilene rolled to a 20-0 halftime lead and played its reserves in the second half.

ON TO THE PLAYOFFS

Abilene was headed for the playoffs for the first time in five years. Up first was a bi-district date with El Paso Austin. Moser won a coin toss, so the game was played at Fair Park Stadium. The crowd was surprisingly small, with only 6,000 in attendance.

Most fans probably thought it was going to be a blowout, as it so often is when teams from the "Little Southwest Conference" face El Paso squads in the playoffs. They were right. Abilene clobbered El Paso Austin, 61-0, in the worst licking Abilene had handed a bi-district opponent since a 95-0 win over Fort Stockton in 1923.

Every back in the game except Briggs, the star of the Midland victory, averaged at least seven yards per carry. Millerman scored three touchdowns, Colwell had 148 yards and two touchdowns on just nine carries, Gregory scored a pair of touchdowns. Bourland tossed a thirty-yard TD pass to Freddie Green, and backup fullback Jack Self scored on a thirty-one-yard run.

In 1954, the playoffs took only three rounds—compared to six today. Fort Worth Poly was the Eagles' next opponent in the semifinals. Abilene continued to roll, beating Poly, 46-0.

Millerman said Moser's amazing ability to dissect an opponent's weaknesses and develop a game plan was never more evident than in the victory over Poly. "I had returned punts all year, and I ran two punts back for touchdowns a week earlier against El Paso. I was feeling pretty good on Monday when Moser called me in his office and said I was going to play linebacker on the punt return team this week. I asked, 'What did I do wrong?' "

"Nothing," Moser answered.

But Moser had noted that Poly used an unusually large split between the center and left guard when it lined up to punt. Moser explained to Millerman that he should be able to block every punt. "So all week I got to practice blocking punts," Millerman said. "Sure enough, when they lined up to punt, it opened up just like he said it would."

Poly's punter shanked his first punt under a heavy Eagle rush. Millerman blocked the second one, and the rout was on.

Cullen Hunt, a starting tackle for the Eagles, also remembers the Fort Worth Poly game, but probably not for the same reason as the rest of his teammates. "I had an older brother and sister living in Fort Worth, so when we played Fort Worth Poly in the semifinals, I had a lot of family there. We had a sweep, and Briggs fumbled. I recovered the fumble. The ball was underneath my chest, and Hawkins landed on me. It took my breath away. They had to take me out of the game because I couldn't get any air. Moser said, 'You're not going to play any more. You'll have to play real good next week.'"

WHAT A GAME

The Eagles entered the state championship game against Stephen F. Austin High School from Houston having outscored their last three opponents, 134-0.

The two teams couldn't agree on a neutral site for the state championship game, and Abilene lost the coin flip, forcing the Eagles to have to play the title contest in Houston. The team flew, while the fans chartered a train for Abilene's first state championship game since 1931.

Those making the long trip weren't disappointed. It was a scintillating football game with a thrilling finish. Ash made a fingertip grab of a pass from Hawkins to score the winning touchdown with fifty-six seconds remaining in a 14-7 victory over the Houston school.

Jack Agness of the *Houston Post* recounted the exciting finish: "Nearly 20,000 spectators in Public School Stadium were resigned to a state co-championship until H.P. Hawkins' 29-yard pass to End Twyman Ash counted in the final minute to break a 7-7 tie. The 6-2 Ash hauled in Hawkins' toss on the five and crossed the corner on a beautifully-executed play to climax a 69-yard last-gasp drive after the East End Mustangs had stalled off the visitors from the westlands through 47 minutes of tremendous football."

Like the Midland game in which Briggs had outshined fullback Wahoo McDaniel, Moser's Eagles beat Stephen F. Austin at its own game. The Mustangs were known for their vaunted passing attack, led by star quarterback Vince Matthews, who went on to play at the University of Texas. But Abilene's defense—led by Hunt, Thomas, Peake, and Bob Hubbard—put a tremendous rush on Matthews, who completed just thirteen of twenty-six passes.

"Besides putting pressure on Matthews, my job was to try to hold up their end, David Webster," Hubbard said. "I did a poor job of that. Actually, that was not one of our better games of the year, but, of course, you probably have to attribute that to the competition. We didn't change anything for that game like we did against Midland and other teams. We lined up in status quo."

The Eagles rolled up 334 yards total offense to just 198 for Austin, but the game was tied going into the fourth quarter.

Abilene had taken a 7-0 lead in the first quarter on Millerman's four-yard run, but Austin recovered an Abilene fumble on the second-half kickoff and turned it into a score, tying the game at 7-7.

The final quarter turned into a nail-biter, twelve minutes of big plays, near misses, and a roller-coaster of emotions. Austin missed a short field-goal try early in the fourth quarter.

A key play to change momentum in Abilene's favor came midway through the final period when the Mustangs were penalized for roughing the kicker as two hard-charging Austin linemen ran into Eagle punter Freddie Green.

"We had changed centers twice in the game," Green recalled. "For some reason, they couldn't get it back to me, but I had been able to get the kick off every time. This time, the ball bounced to me. When I picked it up, I looked up and saw three guys coming right up the middle at me. I just decided to try to kick it."

Somehow Green got the punt off before two Austin defenders crashed into his chest.

"If you look at the film of that game, the ball came out right under the crotch of one of their players," Green said. "If he'd had his legs closed, they would have blocked the punt."

Green's miraculous kick sailed sixty-four yards, but the ball was brought back and Abilene was awarded a first down on the penalty.

Abilene then drove to the one-yard line, but Hawkins fumbled into the end zone and Austin recovered. Abilene held Austin after the fumble, and the Mustangs were forced to punt from deep in their end of the field. Colwell returned the punt fifty-five yards for an

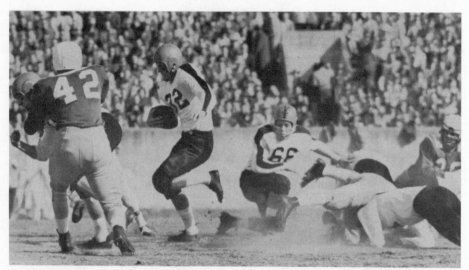

Jimmy Millerman, John Thomas and other Eagles clear the way for Henry Colwell in the Eagles' 1954 state championship game against Houston Austin. (Photo courtesy of Flashlight)

apparent touchdown. A clipping penalty, however, nullified the score, negating another scoring opportunity.

After fifteen yards were walked off for the penalty, the Eagles had possession on their own thirty-one-yard line. That's where the winning drive began.

H.P. Hawkins hooked up with Twyman Ash on passes of thirty-eight and seventeen yards to move the ball to Austin's sixteen-yard line. Hawkins was sacked for a thirteen-yard loss back to the twenty-nine.

On the next play, Hawkins lofted a pass toward Ash, who leaped over the top of the Austin defender, caught the pass, and fell into the end zone with the game-winning score.

"David Webster was the defensive back on the play," Ash recalled. "I got to know him later. He jumped up, but he timed it wrong. I had my hands up. I couldn't see it until it hit my hands. He came down and the ball was right there. I caught it on the five and went into the end zone."

Hawkins never saw Ash make the winning catch. "I was flat on my back. We had been running the same route all day long, hitting

Chuck Moser (right) and assistant Shorty Lawson watch the action on the field as the Eagles clinch their first state championship under Moser in 1954.

Millerman. They picked up Jim, so I glanced to my left. Twyman was the secondary receiver on that play. He had a step on his man, and he had outside position. There wasn't anyone between Twyman and the sideline. I threw it, and then someone decked me."

The headline in the *Houston Post* read, "Abilene needed perfect pass play to whip down Mustangs."

"Six inches either way and Webster would have knocked down that ball," Austin coach Bull Kotrola told the *Post*. "It was a perfect pass. Hawkins threw it to the one spot it had to be. Ash made a great catch. Webster did everything he could to break it up. He was up there, shoulder to shoulder with Ash, but there wasn't anything he could do about getting to that ball."

John Hollis, writing in the *Houston Post*, said: "Ash, a 6-2 youngster with tremendous hands, made like a basketball center in going up for the ball, grabbing it on his fingertips, shaking off Webster and racing the final six yards for the score with 58 seconds remaining in the game. The big fella, in fact, is a basketballer, and a good one. He captains the Abilene basketball team."

As Abilene players celebrated on the sideline, one person didn't participate. Moser was injured on the game-winning play.

"I think it was David Bourland," Moser recalled in the 1988 interview with AISD-TV. "We always had an old bucket with some towels in it on the sideline. With fifty seconds left, H.P. Hawkins threw Twyman Ash a pass. He went up and got the ball and we won the game. When that happened, David Bourland grabbed that bucket and slung it. It hit me right here (above the eye). After the game, some newspaper guys came to the locker room to interview me. All during that interview, Dub Sibley (Abilene's team doctor) was sewing up my eye. Someone sent me a clipping from the *Chicago Tribune*. They had a story about it on the front page that said the only person who was injured in the state championship game was the coach."

Hollis Swafford said the victory over Houston's Stephen F. Austin was the highlight of his high school football career, but for a much different reason.

Twyman Ash (81) made the winning catch in the final minute of the 1954 state championship game to give Abilene High a 14-7 win over Stephen F. Austin High School in Houston. (Photo courtesy of Flashlight)

"I hurt my ankle in the first playoff game against El Paso," Swafford said. "I didn't play against Fort Worth. Then the week we were to play Houston (in the championship), the paper came out and said I wasn't going to start. That really hurt because that was a big thing. We warmed up that day and then went back to the locker room. Moser walked over to me and asked if I could go. I said yes. He said, 'OK, you'll start. But I'll have coaches in the press box watching. If they say you can't go, you're coming out.' I played the whole game. That endeared me to him. He really cared about you."

"I remember everything about the state finals," Millerman said. "Early in the game, I caught a pass down the middle, and they knocked me out. I had never been hurt before. In fact, it was the only time I ever missed a play. Doc Sibley gave me some smelling salts. We

Students enter Fair Park Stadium to see the Eagles in their homecoming game in 1954.

moved on down to the five yard line. I was still a little groggy, but Moser put me back in there. H.P. pitched it to me and I scored the first touchdown. I think Briggs knocked their defensive end all the way into the stands with his lead block in front of me."

Hawkins said his winning touchdown pass to Ash was just one of several key plays in that game. "I fumbled into the end zone, although I still believe I had crossed the goal line before they knocked it out of my hands. Then we had the punt return called back because of a penalty. So we scored three times to get that one touchdown. That's just a reflection of the guys I grew up with. They could have settled for the tie, but they wouldn't be denied."

The Eagles were state champs, and the fun was only beginning. A crowd of 700 attended a banquet at HSU's Rose Field House to honor the state champion Eagles in January. First year Texas A&M coach Bear Bryant was the guest speaker. He drew a big laugh when he noted there were few similarities between the state champs and his team. The Aggies, those who had survived the preseason camp at Junction, won only one game that fall in Bryant's first season.

The Eagle Booster Club gave Moser a new 1955 Buick sedan at the banquet. Varsity assistants Watkins and Groseclose were presented checks for $1,000 each, and JV and sophomore assistant coaches Blackburn, Bullington, Lawson, and Gleaton were rewarded with checks for $400 apiece.

Two weeks later, another banquet was held at Rose Field House. This one was called the "Sixty-Mile Banquet," honoring AAAA state champion Abilene, AAA state champion Breckenridge and Class A runner-up Albany. Breckenridge beat Port Neches, 20-7, in the AAA championship game, while Albany fell 26-6 to Deer Park in the Class A championship tilt. That sixty-mile stretch of highway between Abilene and Breckenridge—which runs through Albany—had produced two state champions and a state runner-up in 1954.

The Abilene newspaper ran a photograph of the first-team all-state selections from the three schools—Ash, Millerman, and Thomas of Abilene, end Sonny Everett and quarterback Bennett Watts of Breckenridge, and fullback Albert Burton of Albany.

Two other Eagles, tackle Cullen Hunt and quarterback Hawkins, were honorable mention selections on the AAAA all-state team.

CHAPTER 6

1955: A Perfect End to a Perfect Season

As football season began in 1955, Tropical Storm Gladys dumped ten and a half inches of rain on Corpus Christi and the Texas Gulf Coast. More rain followed over the next few weeks, causing flooding in some portions of the Big Country, the name given to the rugged country in a hundred-mile radius around Abilene.

The rain brought an end—and at least in some areas—to one of the worst droughts in the region's history. But neither rain nor drought seemed to have any impact on the defending state champion Eagles, who were riding a ten-game winning streak as they entered the 1955 football season.

Abilene opened the new campaign with the look of a state champion, whipping Highland Park, 34-0, in the season opener. Henry Colwell scored two first-quarter touchdowns, and Glynn Gregory, Jimmy Carpenter, and fullback James Welch also scored for the Eagles in the romp over Highland Park.

The next week—September 15—the Texas Interscholastic League, as the governing body of Texas high school athletics was known then, announced a tentative realignment for 1956-57. The TIL (now known as the University Interscholastic League) would expand Class AAAA to sixteen districts. Lubbock, Amarillo, Borger, and Pampa would no longer be included in the district known around the state as the "Little Southwest Conference." The new district would include Abilene, Big Spring, Midland, Odessa, and San Angelo.

That alignment has basically remained intact for nearly fifty years, even with the expansion of additional high schools in Abilene, Midland, and Odessa. The tradition of the same teams playing in the same district for fifty or sixty years is what makes District 3-5A, as it is known today, so different than any other high school district in Texas.

Abilene continued to roll with a 45-20 victory over Sweetwater. Colwell scored on a seventy-six-yard run and Gregory broke free on a thirty-eight-yard TD scamper to give Abilene the early lead against Sweetwater. Colwell added a nine-yard TD run early in the third quarter. Carpenter scored on a four-yard run, and backup quarterback Harold Stephens added a three-yard keeper for a touchdown to bury the Mustangs.

As September came to a close, newspaper headlines focused on the fall of the Peron regime in Argentina and President Eisenhower's heart attack while on a trip to Denver. Heavy rains caused flooding and washed out bridges near Jayton, some eighty miles north of Abilene. In Abilene, the attention was on an October 1 battle with Breckenridge, a rematch with the last team to defeat the Eagles.

It wasn't Abilene's best performance, but the Eagles prevailed, knocking off the Buckaroos, 13-0. Jack Holden wrote about the hometown victory: "A fumbling Abilene Eagle eleven mustered the defense when it counted to take a squeaky 13-0 victory over old rival Breckenridge Friday night, finding the Buckies as they've always been, tough as nails.

"Coach Chuck Moser's Warbirds completed a cycle of thirteen victories in the Fair Park Stadium battle, played before more than 10,000 screaming partisans of the neighboring cities. It was last year that the Buckaroos hung the lone defeat of the season on Abilene. Then both teams went on to scalp everybody else and bring home a state title apiece.

"In losing five of seven fumbles, the Eagles played a little less brilliantly than did the 1954 champs. But they still rolled up 304 yards on the ground and threatened to score three more times than they did."

Colwell scored both touchdowns in the victory over Breckenridge on a five-yard run late in the first quarter and a thirty-seven-yard dash in the third quarter.

Freddie Green and Stuart Peake had key defensive stops for the Eagles, and Sam Caudle, Rufus King, Elmo Cure, and Guy Wells were credited with leading the brilliant defensive performance for Abilene.

That same day, twenty-three-year-old Johnny Podres celebrated his birthday with an 8-3 win for the Brooklyn Dodgers over the New York Yankees in game three of the World Series.

The Yankees had won the first two games, but before the following week was over, the Dodgers had rallied to win the Series, four games to three. Podres blanked the Yankees, 2-0, in game seven, as the Dodgers became the first team to win a best-of-seven series after losing the first two games. It was the Dodgers' first World Series title after having failed so many other times against the Bronx Bombers.

READY FOR DISTRICT

Abilene was preparing for the start of district play. Caudle and Colwell were elected co-captains before the Borger game.

The Eagles made it fourteen wins in a row with a 35-6 victory over Borger. Five different players scored for Abilene—Gregory on a seventeen-yard run, David Bourland on a one-yard sneak, Colwell on a nine-yard run and Carpenter on a five-yard run. Stephens also tossed a thirty-two-yard TD pass to Charles Bradshaw.

Bourland said the Borger game wasn't one of his better performances. "We're sitting in the dressing room before the game when I see Moser walk in and my dad right behind him. I thought, uh-oh. My dad never comes down here before a game." Bourland's sister, who was attending school at North Texas State, had a wreck driving from Denton to Fort Worth and broke her back.

"Coach Moser said later that he debated whether to tell me before the game," Bourland said, "but my dad said there was no debate; he was going to tell me. It was probably the worst game I ever called.

1955 state champions

Luckily, we won. I intercepted a pass and scored a touchdown, but I didn't call a very good game."

Abilene High wasn't the only team with a winning streak. South Junior High, one of two junior high schools feeding the powerful Eagles' program, lost 7-0 to Stamford that week, snapping a thirty-four-game winning streak that dated back to 1951.

One of Moser's coaching gifts was the ability to develop a game plan to surprise his opponents. Case in point was the Eagles' next game against Odessa. It was considered a key showdown since the Eagles were 4-0 and Bronchos 3-0-1 entering the contest.

"All the rumors that week were that Odessa was going to fan its defense out to stop our halfbacks," Caudle said. "But we put in a special trap play for that game, and Jim Welch went seventy-six yards up the middle for a touchdown on the first play of the game. (Center) Elmo Cure and I posted the nose guard, and Stuart (Peake) trapped him. You could have driven a bus through that hole. I can still see Welch's back as he was headed for the end zone."

Colwell had been the offensive star through the first four weeks of the season, but Holden noted the emergence of Welch at fullback in his story about Abilene's surprisingly easy 47-0 romp over Odessa.

Former Abilene High players said the Eagles' black bus struck fear in opponents when it drove into town. (Photo courtesy of Abilene High museum)

"Welch, who scored three touchdowns and mauled Odessa defenses for 233 yards by himself, caught the Bronchos almost completely by surprise. Coach Cooper Robbins' red-shirted giants had expected all their troubles to come from the churning legs of Henry Colwell.

"But Colwell stepped aside to let Welch, who handled the job like an all-stater, move in and with almost perfect line play helped hand the Bronchos their worst defeat in 15 years by an Eagle eleven."

Despite taking a backseat to Welch's remarkable performance, Colwell still rushed for eighty-one yards and two touchdowns.

After the game, Moser said he had never seen a team function with so few mistakes. It was only Abilene's fifth win over Odessa in the last fifteen years.

The Bronchos had been a powerhouse in West Texas, winning the school's only state championship in 1946 and losing to Houston Lamar in the 1953 title game. The 1946 team at Odessa High is probably best remembered for two members of its backfield. The star of the team was running back Byron Townsend, who went on to an outstanding career at the University of Texas and then played for the Los Angeles Rams. The quarterback was Hayden Fry, who played at Baylor and then returned to Odessa to coach. Fry went on to coach at Southern Methodist University, North Texas State, and the University of Iowa. He spent more than twenty years at Iowa, leading the Hawkeyes to three Rose Bowl appearances.

When expansion came several years later to the "Little Southwest Conference" with the addition of a new high school in each city, Odessa High's cross-town rival became the new powerhouse of West Texas. Permian High School appeared in eleven title games and won six state championships in a thirty-year span from 1965-95.

In 1955, however, it was Abilene that earned the reputation as the most formidable foe in West Texas, rolling over Odessa much as Permian did its opponents several decades later.

NOT ENOUGH TICKETS

Abilene ran its win streak to sixteen the next week with a 40-12 victory over Pampa. Gregory scored two of Abilene's six touchdowns on a twenty-eight-yard Statue of Liberty play and a sixty-yard end run. Bourland added a twenty-five-yard keeper for a touchdown and threw a seventy-six-yard TD pass to Butch Adams. Colwell scored on a six-yard run and Welch on a seventy-six-yard run.

A sign of Abilene's remarkable success appeared that week in the *Abilene Reporter-News*, which carried a story about fans' complaints that there weren't enough tickets available at Fair Park Stadium. Four years later, Abilene moved into a new stadium. It was eventually named for Pete Shotwell, but the new stadium was built thanks to the success of Moser's teams.

Amarillo was next on Abilene's schedule, and this game was an interesting match-up because of the Sandies' new coach. A year earlier, Joe Kerbel had been coaching at Breckenridge, handing the Eagles their only loss of the season. After winning a state title at Breckenridge in 1954, Kerbel left to take over the Amarillo program.

Kerbel's Sandies put up a good fight, but they were no match for the talented Eagles. Abilene won the game 35-13, oddly enough the identical score of the Eagles' loss to Breckenridge a year earlier:

Big plays were the difference in the game. Gregory rushed for 220 yards on fourteen carries, scoring on runs of fifty-three, ten, and sixty-nine yards. He also kicked all five extra points.

Abilene was starting to hit its stride, just as it had done a year earlier. After the victory over Amarillo, the Eagles followed with impressive wins over Lubbock, Midland, and San Angelo to close out the regular season.

Win number eighteen in a row came on a Saturday afternoon at Texas Tech's Jones Stadium as the Eagles whipped Lubbock, 62-7.

"I got credit for a big play against Lubbock, but Sam Caudle did all the work," Peake said. "Sam had gotten his face mask broken a couple of times by E.J. Holub in that game. On defense, I played right defensive end, and Sam played linebacker behind me. When they lined up to punt, Sam told me that he could beat that man. He broke to the outside and I went to the inside and blocked the punt. We were off-sides, though. But the five yards didn't give them a first down, so they had to kick again. Sam said, 'I'll take him inside,' so I went outside and blocked the kick again. But it was all Sam's deal."

Abilene owned a 35-0 advantage by halftime and made it 42-0 on the first possession of the third quarter. The subs played the rest of the way. The Eagles' first team failed to score on only one possession in the first three periods.

"Coming back on the bus, we were whooping and hollering," Rufus King said. "Moser stood up and said, 'I don't know why you're feeling so good.' He said that was the sorriest blocking and tackling he'd ever seen. He was a master psychologist. He never let you think you were getting too good."

WAHOO vs. GREGORY

Once again, the game against Midland and its powerful fullback Wahoo McDaniel would decide the district championship. The Eagles won their nineteenth game in a row and clinched at least a tie for the title with a 28-7 win over the Bulldogs. Holden wrote: "As great as Midland's steamrolling Wahoo McDaniel was, Abilene had a man

Fullback James Welch finds an opening and races for a touchdown in the 1955 state championship game against Tyler. (Photo courtesy of Flashlight)

on the field who equaled or bettered the Choctaw's vicious charges. Glynn Gregory scored two touchdowns, had another called back and booted four perfect extra points."

Holden called the win over Midland "Abilene's toughest game since the 1954 title game." Cure and Homer Rosenbaum fell on a fumble in the end zone for a touchdown, and Bourland scored on a four-yard keeper in the fourth quarter for the Eagles' other two scores.

"I intercepted two passes and we beat them for the district championship," Caudle said. "Their quarterback, Larry Cooper, went on to play at Texas. Their coach, Tugboat Jones, later went to Highland Park. Wahoo was hard to tackle. You'd hit him and then hang on until help got there."

Thanksgiving Day brought the traditional regular-season finale against San Angelo. The Eagles needed a victory to win their second straight outright district championship. They got it with a 35-6 romp over the Bobcats, thanks to an amazing performance from Gregory.

Holden noted Gregory's performance and remarkable versatility in his story in the local paper: "With the Eagles' great halfback Glynn Gregory intercepting three passes, scoring two touchdowns and kicking five extra points, Abilene hurdled the last barrier and took its second straight District 1-AAAA championship Thursday afternoon at Fair Park Stadium."

For the second year in a row, Abilene had run the table against its tough District 1-AAAA competition, and the winning streak had reached twenty in a row as the Eagles prepared for the playoffs.

Abilene was certainly riding a hot streak, having outscored its seven district opponents by a combined score of 282-51. The Eagles weren't just winning football games; they were overwhelming their opponents.

HUGE PLAYOFF MARGINS

Abilene opened the playoffs with a bi-district game in El Paso. A year earlier, the Eagles had dominated El Paso Austin, 61-0, at Fair Park Stadium. This time, the Warbirds had to go to El Paso to take on El Paso High. The outcome was exactly the same as the 1954 playoff game as Abilene beat the Tigers, 61-0.

Colwell ripped off a fifty-one-yard run for a touchdown on the Eagles' first play from scrimmage. Gregory went fifty-seven yards for a score on the next series, and it was 34-0 by the end of the first quarter and 48-0 by halftime.

The Eagles had a home game in the semifinals as they took on Dallas Sunset. The Abilene defense held Sunset running back Robert Robinson to just thirty-four yards in the first half. Welch carried the load offensively for the Eagles, as noted in Holden's game story in the *Reporter-News:*

"With fullback James Welch tearing up the Sunset line for four touchdowns and 101 yards, Abilene's powerful Eagles rolled right past the Bisons, 33-6, Saturday and into the state finals for the seventh time in history.

"Despite 49-degree weather and a chilling 30-mile north wind, an estimated 9,500 fans turned out to watch the Fair Park rivalry."

Glynn Gregory (21) takes off around left end against San Angelo as quarterback David Bourland fakes that he still has the football. (Photo courtesy of Flashlight)

Welch had nineteen carries, an unusually large total for an individual back on a Moser-coached team. Welch's longest run was only fifteen yards for a third-quarter touchdown, but the senior fullback consistently gained four or five yards. Bourland threw an eighty-three-yard TD pass to Gregory for Abilene's other score.

UNDERDOGS!

Incredibly, the defending state champion Eagles, riding a twenty-two-game winning streak, were considered underdogs against Tyler in the state championship game, which was scheduled for TCU's Amon Carter Stadium in Fort Worth.

Tyler was also unbeaten, and the Lions featured 6-3, 195-pound all-state quarterback Charlie Milstead, who was named the state's player of the year in 1955.

Some 7,000 fans from Abilene, including 900 who went by train, made the 150-mile trip to Fort Worth to see the Eagles go for a second straight state championship. What they saw has since been described as the closest thing to a perfect game a football team could play.

"There was so much hype about how good Charlie Milstead and Tyler was," Bullington recalled. "It was played at Amon Carter Stadium in front of 30,000 people. It was out of hand in the second half. We played everybody."

Holden's story the next day in the Abilene paper cited the remarkable performance displayed by the Eagles: "With the swiftness of lightning, perfect timing and flawless blocking, the Abilene Eagles Saturday for the fifth time in history joined the ranks of state football champions.

"Here at TCU's friendly stadium in warm sunshine and with some 25,000 or more looking on, Coach Chuck Moser's great Warbirds repeated as state Class AAAA champs. The victim was Tyler, 33-13, and so business-like was the execution of the Lions that this victory seemed as simple as the 12 which preceded it this season.

"This one belongs to Abilene's line which did its job so perfectly that Tyler was never in the ball game. From the very first play it was clear that the Eagles were not to be denied. When the two hours of domination was complete, they joined the heroes of 1923, 1928, 1931, and 1954 in Abilene's special hall of fame.

"Despite their 22 straight victories in previous games, the Eagles never performed like this. The backs, Glynn Gregory, Henry Colwell, James Welch and David Bourland, played the champions' role to perfection."

Gregory led Abilene with 171 yards rushing on sixteen carries. He scored on a forty-yard Statue of Liberty play and a four-yard run. Welch added a pair of scores and Colwell one touchdown for the Eagles. Abilene's running attack—led by Gregory, Welch and Colwell—gained 351 yards, while the entire Tyler team had only seventy-two yards rushing and passing, most of that against the Abilene substitutes.

GREATEST IN HISTORY

Harold Ratliff, who spent more than thirty years as the Texas sports editor for the Associated Press bureau in Dallas, said in his book—*Autum's Mightiest Legions*, a history of Texas high school football—that the 1955 Abilene team "was generally regarded as the greatest in Texas schoolboy football history."

Abilene, he wrote, "played as nearly perfect football—blocking, tackling, precision offense, impregnable defense—as could be hoped for" against Tyler. "(Abilene) drove 95, 90 and 80 yards for touchdowns to lead 20-0 at the half. It ran up a 33-0 score before Moser put in his reserves."

Even in the state championship game, Moser wouldn't let his team relax with a big lead. "We were way ahead at halftime," Rufus King said. "We were in the locker room at halftime and Butch Adams, who died a year after we got out of school, got up to get a drink of water. Moser jumped all over him. He did that just to keep us from getting too cocky."

Tyler didn't score its two touchdowns until the fourth quarter against the Eagles' reserves.

Moser, in typical fashion, praised his players and assistant coaches in his post-game comments.

"Hank (Watkins) did a tremendous job with our line in setting the strategy to stop Tyler's option stuff," Moser said, "and Blacky (Blackburn) and Wally (Bullington) really had them scouted. We thought if (Guy) Wells and (Stuart) Peake could keep Milstead inside on that option stuff and Elmo Cure, Rufus King, and Bufford Carr could stop them up the middle, we'd be in pretty good shape. Hank worked with those ends all week and really did a tremendous job, while Wally worked with our guards and linebackers."

Bourland, who had a nearly perfect day of play calling, said after the game that he was "sick and tired of reading about Milstead."

Milstead, held to just thirteen yards on fourteen carries and completing only two passes for twenty-three yards, had nothing but praise for Abilene following the loss to the Eagles. "The Lions could

Glynn Gregory (21) races for one of his two touchdowns in the 1955 state championship game against Tyler. He had 171 yards rushing in the game for the Eagles. (Photo courtesy of Flashlight)

play Abilene every day of the week and never beat 'em," said Milstead, who went on to star at Texas A&M. "They were twice as good as we thought they were."

Asked for the key to the game, Milstead said "the opening kickoff."

Actually, Abilene fumbled the opening kickoff. But the Eagles, pinned against their own goal line, marched ninety-five yards on the game's first possession to score and set the tone for the remainder of the afternoon.

"We put in a special trap play, the 'Tyler Special', for that game," Peake said. "Glynn (Gregory) slipped and fumbled on the opening kickoff, so we started out at our own five-yard line. I think we ran an off-tackle play on first down. Then we called the 'Tyler Special,' and Gregory went all the way."

Bourland said Moser usually called the first play of the game ahead of time, but this time he called the first two plays. The off-tackle play was designed to set up the "Tyler Special" on second down.

"It was a trap play," Gregory said of the "Tyler Special." "Moser said we'll do this and they'll react this way. This is how and why it will work. After I got through the line of scrimmage, I had to run parallel to the line. That gave another player the angle, and I couldn't out-run him." By the time Gregory was dragged down, however, he had gained more than forty yards and Abilene was out of a hole and on

Tyler's end of the field, preparing to score the game's first touchdown.

The Eagles wore their traditional gold jerseys that day, but Moser had had other thoughts.

"For some reason, Coach Moser bought new jerseys for that state championship game," Bourland said. "He told us at a quarterback meeting that week. They were white. I looked at him funny, and he asked what was wrong. I said, 'You wear the same shirt every week because you're superstitious. We've been winning in our gold jerseys.'"

"You're right," Moser said. "Forget it."

The Abilene Eagles never took the field in their "new" white jerseys.

MORE TO COME

A week later, Abilene was host to the Class AA state championship game. Wood's Stamford Bulldogs won their first of two straight titles with a 34-7 win over Hillsboro. Oddly enough, by agreement of the two coaches, the game was played on Monday, December 26, in front of a packed Fair Park Stadium. It may very well be the only state championship football game in Texas schoolboy history played after Christmas.

Five days later, 1955 came to an end. The decade of the '50s had reached the midway point, but the Abilene Eagles were far from finished. The winning streak was twenty-three. There were still more victories and another state championship to win as the legend of the "Team of the Century" continued.

Three more Eagles—end Freddie Green, guard Sam Caudle, and running back Glynn Gregory—were all-state selections on offense, making it two years in a row that Abilene had placed three players on the all-state first team. Caudle was also named fourth team on the All-American High School Football Team. Honorable mention all-state recognition was given to center Elmo Cure and backs Henry Colwell and David Bourland.

Abilene Christian graduate and former ACC coach Tonto Coleman, the assistant athletic director at Georgia Tech, was the guest speaker at the Eagles' football banquet at Rose Field House. Coleman told the crowd of 700 in attendance that "outside of the church, the football coach does more for the youth of a city than anyone. He wields the greatest influence."

Nowhere was that more apparent than in Abilene.

The Eagle Booster Club presented checks totaling $7,950 to the coaching staff, including $3,000 for Moser and $1,500 for Hank Watkins, his top assistant.

Moser noted some of the Eagles' remarkable accomplishments during his comments at the banquet:

- Two straight state championships
- Twenty-three consecutive victories
- One loss in the last thirty games
- 501 points scored last season
- 948 points scored in the past two years
- Only one blocked punt in two years
- No run by an opponent of longer than fifteen yards in the last twenty-three games
- No pass completed over a player's head in the last eighteen games.

Abilene was the king of Texas high school football, and the Eagles weren't about to be knocked off their pedestal anytime soon. With twenty-three consecutive victories at the end of 1955 season, Abilene's amazing win streak hadn't even reached its midway point yet.

More victories—and championships—were yet to come.

CHAPTER 7

1956: Three in a Row

As practice began for the 1956 football season, newspapers were filled with stories of riots and violence in battles over school integration, both in Texas and elsewhere around the country. It was obvious that the winds of change were starting to blow.

A name change was also announced on September 6. The new Abilene Air Force Base would now be known as Dyess Air Force Base, named in honor of the late Lt. Col. Eddie Dyess of Albany.

But not everything was changing. Abilene was still the king of Texas high school football. The Eagles, winners of two straight state championships and twenty-three consecutive games, were the preseason favorites to make it three in a row in 1956. A panel of high school coaches picked Abilene to win state again. The Eagles received fourteen of sixteen first-place votes. Baytown and Pasadena garnered the other two votes.

Despite the lofty expectations, Abilene returned only three starters on offense—Glynn Gregory at running back, Stuart Peake at guard, and Rufus King, who moved from tackle to end. King and Peake were elected team captains.

The opening-day lineup included Kenny Schmidt and King at ends, Bufford Carr and Boyd King at tackles, Peake and Guy Wells at guards, Jim Rose at center, Harold "Hayseed" Stephens at quarterback, Gregory and Jimmy Carpenter at halfbacks, and Charles Bradshaw at fullback.

For the first time in the Moser Era, Abilene opened the season against an opponent other than Dallas Highland Park. San Antonio Edison provided the new competition, but the result was the same as the Eagles romped, 41-6.

Don Oliver, who had replaced Jack Holden as sports editor of the *Abilene Reporter-News* since the previous football season, covered the season opener:

"Coach Chuck Moser used some new ingredients, but the results were completely satisfying to some 10,500 fans at Fair Park Stadium Friday night as the defending Class AAAA state champion Eagles crushed Edison of San Antonio, 41-6, in the 1956 debut and notched their 24th straight win."

Moser played the subs in the second half. Edison didn't score its only touchdown until the final minute of the game. Reserve back Chuck Colvin scored three touchdowns for Abilene.

Abilene made it twenty-five in a row with a surprisingly easy 39-7 win over Sweetwater, a team that had typically played the Eagles close.

Mistakes were costly for the Mustangs in this one. Sweetwater fumbled on the game's opening possession. Two plays later, Abilene scored on Charles Bradshaw's seven-yard run. Bradshaw scored again on an eleven-yard run as the Eagles grabbed a 12-0 halftime lead. Abilene then pulled away in the second half, taking advantage of the Mustangs' miscues.

Women's sports were almost non-existent in 1956 and certainly didn't receive much recognition in the local newspaper. But on September 27, the day that Abilene was scheduled to face Lubbock Monterey, the lead story on the sports pages was the death of Babe Didrikson Zaharias, still considered one of the greatest female athletes of all time. Didrikson Zaharias, who was an Olympic track athlete and professional golf star, lost her battle with cancer and died at age forty-two in Galveston.

That night, the Eagles faced Monterey, Lubbock's new high school, at Jones Stadium. The winless Plainsmen were no match for Abilene. *Reporter-News* writer Jimmy Browder covered the Eagles' twenty-sixth consecutive victory: "Coach Chuck Moser could have named any score from one to 100 Friday night and his Eagles probably would have achieved it."

Abilene led 35-0 at halftime and played the second and third teams in the second half, settling for a 41-0 finale. Hayseed Stephens completed all five passes that he attempted for 117 yards.

EMORY BELLARD

Week four brought an old rival but a new coach. The Eagles faced Breckenridge, under the leadership of Emory Bellard, who would go on to make quite a name for himself. After coaching at Breckenridge, Bellard guided San Angelo to a state championship. He then became the offensive coordinator for Darrell Royal at the University of Texas, where he was credited with inventing the wishbone offense. Later he served as head coach at Texas A&M and Mississippi State.

But on the first Friday night of October 1956, Bellard's young Buckaroos were no match for Abilene, which was making a habit of jumping on its opponents early. The Eagles blanked Breckenridge, 41-0, the same score as the Monterey game a week earlier.

Jimmy Carpenter scored on runs of thirteen, eighteen, and thirty-three yards, while Gregory's touchdown runs came from twenty-nine and forty-seven yards out. Gregory rushed for 146 yards on just six carries, and Carpenter gained ninety-one yards on the ground as Abilene amassed 310 of its 383 yards of total offense in the first half.

Just three days after the Eagles' lopsided win over Breckenridge—the last team to beat them two years earlier—one of the greatest events in sports history took place. New York Yankees pitcher Don Larsen hurled the first—and only—perfect game in World Series history on Monday, October 8, as the Yankees beat the Brooklyn Dodgers, 2-0, to take a three games to two lead in the Series.

As the sports world buzzed about Larsen's gem, Abilene prepared to take on Lubbock High, the team the Eagles had supplanted as the king of West Texas football. Abilene had become so dominant that the running joke around town was that several Eagles would be named all-state but wouldn't letter because they hadn't played enough minutes in Abilene's lopsided victories. Don Oliver noted in his daily column in the *Reporter-News* that all four of the starters in the backfield—Stephens, Gregory, Carpenter, and Bradshaw—had played in less than half the minutes through the first four games of the season.

Lubbock High, meanwhile, had fallen on hard times, just three years after winning the 1952 state championship. The opening of a new school, injuries, and a change in coaching staffs had left the Westerners with only twenty-eight players on the varsity roster. Lubbock star E.J. Holub had injured his knee earlier in the year against Odessa and was out for the rest of the season. It would be just the beginning of knee problems for Holub, who had his knees operated on seventeen times before his pro football career ended.

Although he missed the rest of the 1956 high school season, Holub went on to play football at Texas Tech and then had a lengthy professional career with the Kansas City Chiefs. In fact, Holub is the only player in Super Bowl history to start on both offense and defense. He was a starting linebacker for the Chiefs in their loss to the Green Bay Packers in the first Super Bowl and then was the Chiefs' starting center when Kansas City upset the Minnesota Vikings in Super Bowl IV.

Wilford Moore, the former McMurry University head coach, had returned to coaching at Lubbock High after a year's absence from the profession. Moore's name is now associated with the trophy given to the winner of the cross-town football game in Abilene between Hardin-Simmons and McMurry. Moore played at Hardin-Simmons and later coached at McMurry and is the only person who is a member of both schools' hall of fame.

But in 1956, Moore was at Lubbock High. He knew going into the game that his Westerners were no match for the team coached by his good friend Chuck Moser.

"I really hate to come back down there this week," Moore told Oliver in his October 9 column in the Abilene newspaper. "I wouldn't mind it if we had a good team, one that would play Chuck a good game—but we don't have. Man, they'll hit us so hard Friday night our kids won't be able to focus their eyes on the Texas-OU game on television Saturday afternoon."

Moore was right. Abilene whipped his Westerners, 49-7.

Stephens threw only two passes, but he completed both of them for touchdowns of forty-seven and forty-six yards to Gregory, who also had a twenty-seven-yard TD run. Carpenter had a ninety-four-yard punt return and a forty-eight-yard scoring run from scrimmage. Fullback Bill Sides scored on an eighty-one-yard run on a fake pass with two seconds left in the half.

WACO IS NO MATCH

A new opponent, Waco, was next on the Eagles' schedule. The pregame stories in the local paper centered on the renewal of the rivalry between the two schools and the Eagles' winning streak that was about to reach record proportions. The Class AAAA record for consecutive wins was twenty-nine, set by Lubbock in 1951-53. A victory over Waco would give Abilene a share of that record.

Waco and Abilene played each other three times in state championship games in the 1920s, but hadn't faced each other since. It had been twenty-nine years since the Tigers and Eagles had met on a football field. Waco legend Boody Johnson drop-kicked a game-winning field goal to give the Tigers a 10-7 win over Abilene in the 1922 state championship game. The Eagles returned the favor the next year, winning the 1923 title game, 3-0, on Pete Hanna's twenty-three-yard field goal. Hanna, Dub Wooten, and Bob Estes—grandfather of the PGA Tour golfer by the same name—were among the stars of Abilene's first state championship team. The two teams met for a third time in a state championship game in 1927, with Waco winning 27-14.

In 1956, however, Waco was no match for Abilene. The Eagles ran only seventeen offensive plays in the first half but still grabbed a 29-

7 advantage en route to a 45-14 victory over the Tigers. Gregory had seventy-two yards rushing on just five carries and caught both of Stephens' passes for a total of 122 yards and two touchdowns. Carpenter had five carries for fifty-three yards and scored three touchdowns. Colvin had eight carries for fifty-three yards, and Reyes Diaz ran for fifty yards on seven attempts.

Abilene had tied the state record with twenty-nine wins in a row, but the Eagles were doing more than just winning. They were demolishing the competition. During the winning streak, Abilene had averaged 38.8 points per game while allowing their opponents just 5.9. The Eagles had outscored their opponents 1,111 to 173 since that loss to Breckenridge in the third game of the 1954 season. Sweetwater was the only team to score three touchdowns in a game against Abilene (in 1955) during the streak, and only five teams scored two touchdowns in a game against the Eagles. Abilene had shut out ten of its twenty-nine victims so far.

The Eagles weren't finished, however. Amazingly, the streak was only a little past its halfway point, although no one could have known that in October 1956.

THIRTY IN A ROW

Abilene opened district play against Big Spring, the newest member of 2-AAAA. The Eagles' thirtieth win in a row looked a lot like many of the others. The Eagles turned three fumbles by the Steers and a sixty-one-yard punt return by Gregory into a 35-0 first-quarter lead. The subs played the rest of the way as Abilene welcomed Big Spring to the district with a 42-6 thumping.

The presidential election topped the headlines as the Eagles prepared for a key district game with Odessa High. President Dwight Eisenhower won re-election on November 7, beating Adlai Stevenson in a rematch of the 1952 race. Stevenson took fourteen of twenty counties in the Big Country area surrounding Abilene, a region that traditionally voted Democratic. But the Eisenhower-Nixon ticket carried Taylor County 8,167 to 6,574. Texas voted for Ike by an even larger margin than in 1952, and Eisenhower carried every state except Montana and six states in the South. The headline the next morning in the *Abilene Reporter-News* read: "Ike Sweeps to Mighty Win."

Replace "Ike" with "Eagles," and the headline would have been appropriate for every Abilene football game in 1956. The Warbirds were rolling over opponents, and next up was Odessa High, led by former Broncho and second-year head coach Hayden Fry.

Guard Ervin Bishop recovered a fumble at the thirteen-yard line on Odessa's first possession of the game. Seconds later, Carpenter scored on a three-yard run and the Eagles were off and running to a 47-6 victory, increasing the streak to thirty-one.

The Odessa victory was another example of Moser's tremendous preparation. Bullington said the scouts had seen the Bronchos line up in the swinging gate formation a week earlier, but the opposing team had called timeout before Odessa could run the play. After the timeout, the Bronchos switched plays and didn't run the unusual spread formation. When the scouts told Moser that, he said, "I bet they're running the 'Oklahoma Swinging Gate.'"

Bullington said Moser called Oklahoma coach Bud Wilkinson and had him explain what the Sooners do on the play. Sure enough, Odessa tried the trickery against the Eagles that Friday night, but Moser's team was prepared. "We knew what they were going to do better than the Odessa players did," Bullington said.

Gregory scored on touchdown runs of thirty-one and sixty-six yards, and Carpenter on runs of three, fifty-five, and forty yards for Abilene. Colvin also returned an interception forty-five yards for a touchdown.

Midland, led by fullback Wahoo McDaniel, had provided Abilene with its toughest district game the past two years. But McDaniel had moved on to the University of Oklahoma and the Bulldogs were no match for Abilene.

The Eagles, however, led just 14-0 at halftime, their lowest total of the year. "We were up 7-0, and I took a pitchout from Hayseed and barely scored (on a four-yard run) right before half to go up 14-0,"

Carpenter recalled. "Moser was not happy. That was the worst chewing out we ever had."

Moser's halftime lecture obviously worked as Abilene went on to drub Midland, 41-6, scoring on six of its eight remaining possessions. The Eagles had only three starters in the lineup when Midland scored its touchdown.

SHOWDOWN WITH SAN ANGELO

Abilene had averaged 42.3 points per game in its first nine games. Next up was the regular-season finale against San Angelo, a matchup of number one vs. number two in the state. Both teams were 9-0, and an overflow crowd was expected at Fair Park to see the 1956 "Game of the Century."

As Abilene prepared for its traditional Thanksgiving Day game with San Angelo, Oliver wrote in his column that Abilene needed a new football stadium. Fair Park Stadium was no longer large enough to hold the crowds for the three biggest games of the year—Abilene vs. San Angelo, Hardin-Simmons vs. Texas Tech, and Abilene Christian vs. McMurry. Noting that San Angelo had sold bonds to build a new stadium, Oliver called for Abilene to build a 25,000-seat stadium.

Thanksgiving Day was also the first time that the *Abilene Reporter-News* made reference to an unusual shirt that Moser wore to each game. Writing in his daily column, Oliver talked about Moser's good-luck shirt: "That 'orange-pinkish' colored shirt you'll see on Abilene High Coach Chuck Moser this afternoon isn't the only shirt the successful young mentor has, although he has worn it to Eagle games ever since the first (playoff) game of 1955 against El Paso High. 'I'm not superstitious,' Moser explains, 'it's just that I don't want to change anything.' The shirt was given to him by his Sunday School class three years ago and has been his good-luck talisman."

Doris Moser called the shirt "salmon pink." Chuck said he wouldn't wear pink, and he wouldn't wear orange because that was San Angelo's color. "I guess you call it orangish-pink," Moser said. A year later, a story in the local paper called Moser's good-luck shirt a "watermelon" color.

Christine Smith was crowned homecoming queen that day, and the Eagles blanked previously unbeaten San Angelo, 20-0, to close out the regular season. The real story of the victory over Bobcats was the Abilene High defense. Sports writer Fred Sanner noted that the Eagles' defense shut out a previously unbeaten San Angelo team that had been averaging thirty-one points a game:

"The same numbers—74, 23, 66, 60, 36, 53, 70, 72, 29 and 64—piled up play after play, as tackle Rufus King, halfback Charles Bradshaw, end Ervin Bishop, linebacker Guy Wells, end Stuart Peake, linebacker Jim Rose, tackles Boyd King and Bufford Carr, halfback Gervis Galbraith, and John Young baffled the Bobcat offense," Sanner wrote.

Although the win gave Abilene a third consecutive undefeated regular season and another post-season berth, Sanner noted that the Eagles' victory did not come without a cost: "Lost to Coach Chuck Moser's defending state champions was quarterback Harold (Hayseed) Stephens, who suffered a broken leg in the fourth quarter after he had guided the Warbirds to a 20-0 lead."

Starting lineman Guy Wells also suffered a kidney injury in the game.

"We were big rivals, and that was a brutal, tough game," Carpenter said. "I've never been hit harder than I was in that San Angelo game."

Carpenter remembers the San Angelo game for another reason. "I had an abscessed tooth, and it was killing me. For some reason, they didn't want to pull it. Dr. Nichols (an Abilene dentist) was on the bench, and he kept giving me a shot to numb it. San Angelo pounded us, and by the time the game was over I was worn out. It was Thanksgiving afternoon, but right after the game my girlfriend took me to the dentist's office and he pulled my tooth."

What impact would Stephens' broken leg have on the Eagles' chances for a third straight championship? That was the talk the next day after the victory over San Angelo. It was such an issue that Don Oliver devoted his entire column to the topic, including an interview with Stephens from his hospital bed.

"One guy being out won't stop our ball club," Stephens told Oliver. "There isn't one guy on the squad they couldn't get along without, unless maybe it'd be Greg or Carp. Shoot, if they'll make up their minds and get determined, they can go all the way. That's what football is, the team that is the most determined is going to win. And a man like Chuck Moser can pull anything out of the fire."

GOLD MEDAL WINNER

Another Abilene resident was making headlines as the Eagles prepared for their bi-district playoff game against El Paso Ysleta. Half a world away, Abilene Christian College sprinter Bobby Morrow was becoming an American hero, winning three gold medals at the Olympics in Melbourne, Australia.

Morrow, who grew up in San Benito in the Rio Grande Valley, won the 100 and 200 and ran on the Americans' winning 400-meter relay team. Meanwhile, his wife JoAnn was named homecoming queen at ACC.

One of the myths that has evolved over the years is that the Eagles, missing their quarterback, won the state championship in 1956 without throwing a pass in the playoffs. That's not true, but Moser probably did become a little more conservative as he tried to find the right replacement for Stephens.

He moved Gregory to quarterback for the Eagles' 42-6 win over Ysleta. Oliver wrote:

"After being thwarted the first two times they got the ball, the Warbirds went for touchdowns the next five times to rack up a comfortable 35-0 halftime advantage, and reserves more than held their own against the Redskins the rest of the way.

"Glynn Gregory engineered the first four Warbird markers before returning to his old left half slot to let Gervis Galbraith run the methodical Abilene express. Freddie Martinez, brought up from the B team at the end of the season, was at the throttle most of the third and fourth periods."

Notre Dame's Golden Boy, Paul Hornung, was named the winner of the Heisman Trophy on the same day that Abilene faced Fort

Worth Paschal in the second round of the playoffs at Farrington Field in Fort Worth.

Gregory quarterbacked the first half and Galbraith the second half. The two were a combined zero for seven passing, but the lack of an air attack in the Eagles' 14-0 win over Paschal may have had more to do with the weather than a lack of emphasis on the passing game, according to Oliver in his game story in the *Reporter-News*:

"With a blanket-covered crowd of 10,000 braving 36-degree weather, misting rain and drifting snowflakes that tumbled down during the fourth period, Glynn Gregory and a stubborn Warbird defense combined to draw the curtain on Paschal's 'Cinderella team' that had hopes of going all the way after upsetting Amarillo last week.

"Gregory was the individual hero, if one was to be picked, although Coach Chuck Moser's line was near perfect. Stuart Peake, Jimmy Rose, Rufus King, Ervin Bishop, Gerald Galbraith, Bufford Carr, and Boyd King repulsed the Panther backs and combined to hold Paschal to a net of only 41 yards rushing for the game."

Paschal never crossed the fifty-yard line the entire game, finally reaching its own forty-seven in the fourth quarter before Carpenter intercepted a pass to end the "threat."

"It was sleeting," Rufus King said. "That was one game you didn't want to come out. It was cold on that bench."

Peake also remembered a trick play in the Paschal game. "Moser always tried to do something to confuse teams. He decided to put in a few single-wing plays against Paschal, just so our next opponent would have to waste time preparing for it. Paschal had an outstanding linebacker named Roy Lee Rambo. When we lined up in the single-wing, he started calling out signals, and then he shouted, 'What the 'f—-" is this?' We'd never heard anyone talk like that, and we all started laughing. We thought Moser was going to kill us because we were laughing so hard we couldn't snap the ball."

As the Eagles prepared for their semifinal match with Wichita Falls, Abilene took time to celebrate another sports hero as Morrow returned to town. A front-page picture on December 12 featured Morrow with ACC track coach Oliver Jackson. Several Texas sports legends, including former Texas A&M running back John Kimbrough, pro golfer Byron Nelson, and baseball Hall of Famer Tris Speaker, were among those speaking at a testimonial dinner honoring him.

Meanwhile, Moser named Galbraith his quarterback for the remainder of the playoffs, allowing Gregory to move back to halfback. It was a good move, as Gregory and halfback mate Carpenter led the Eagles to a 20-6 victory over Wichita Falls.

Each team threw only four passes—and failed to complete any—as the two teams battled it out on the ground. Carpenter rushed for eighty-four yards on seventeen carries, scoring on runs of nineteen and five yards, while Gregory had twenty-six carries for 131 yards and a fourteen-yard TD run. The Eagles made it thirty-six in a row, heading into a showdown with Corpus Christi Ray for the state championship.

"Wichita Falls ran a single wing," defensive tackle Rufus King remembered. "The defensive line's job was to penetrate and start grabbing arms and legs. That was a lot of fun, but the linebackers made all the tackles."

"Moser defended the single wing better than anyone," said Jim Rose, who played middle linebacker in the Eagles' defense. "I probably made 30 tackles against Wichita Falls. I never was blocked. But that was the only time I can remember that we had a punt returned for a touchdown against us. I never saw Moser madder than that. It happened right before half. Erwin Bishop missed a tackle. I think he's a Church of Christ preacher now. The reason may be because he saw God that day."

Peake remembers a trick play that Moser devised for Wichita Falls. "Moser dreamed up the three-flip. I was supposed to split out real wide, about five yards from the center (Rose). Then we'd flip it to the opposite back on a sweep. We called the play and I scooted out. Well, (the defensive player) moved out with me, so I moved out a little more. Finally, he took the bait and moved in closer to Rose. We scored on the play, and after the game (Oklahoma coach) Bud Wilkinson came into the locker room and asked Moser what in the hell was that play?"

CHAMPIONSHIP GAME

Memorial Stadium on the University of Texas campus in Austin was the site for the 1956 Class AAAA state championship game. Abilene was gunning for its third straight state title, a feat that had been accomplished only twice in the state's top classification—by Waco (1925-27) and Amarillo (1934-36)—and once since (Midland Lee 1998-2000).

Carpenter turned in a brilliant performance, leading Abilene to a 14-0 victory over Corpus Christi Ray. Oliver wrote: "Dazzling little Jimmy Carpenter put on one of the greatest one-man shows in the history of Texas schoolboy football here Saturday afternoon as he led the Abilene Eagles into the Class AAAA throne room for the third straight year.

"The 153-pounder who refused to go down scored both touchdowns on runs of 94 and 62 yards as the Warbirds trimmed Corpus Christi Ray, 14-0, before 17,000 sun-baked fans to move alongside Waco and Amarillo as the only schools ever winning three state championships in a row.

"Carpenter, a two-time All-State baseball outfielder, gained 227 yards on 16 carries for a 14.2 average and two touchdowns and played a tremendous defensive game, intercepting two Ray passes from his safety slot.

"Sharing the honors was Glynn Gregory with 71 yards in 20 trips and a stout-hearted Eagle defensive platoon headed by Gerald Galbraith, Rufus King, Boyd King, Bufford Carr, Stuart Peake and Jimmy Rose.

"Actually the defenders may have had more to do with the victory than it seems, for they rose up to stop the Texans on the Eagle one-foot stripe on their first offensive series and that might have taken the steam out of the Corpus Christians."

Ray coach Bill Stages agreed that Abilene's goal-line stand in the first quarter may have been the difference in the game.

The Texans took the game's opening possession and quickly drove into scoring position, reaching first-and-goal at the four-yard line. Ray quarterback Arthur McCallum gained two yards on first down. Bart Shirley dove to the one-yard line on second down. McCallum tried another sneak on third down, but he was stopped a foot short of the goal line.

That brought up the critical fourth-down play.

"We held them on the first three plays, but the nose of the ball was just short of the goal line," recalled Rose. "I was lined up in the middle of our goal-line defense, and I didn't think we could stop them from scoring so I was just going to punish the center. Rufus (King) said the same thing about the guard in front of him."

Apparently the fear factor worked. Ray fumbled the exchange between quarterback and center, and Gerald Galbraith recovered the fumble at the three-yard line. McCallum said he didn't know what happened; he never received the exchange from all-state center Max Christian.

"I think he pulled out too quick," Galbraith said of Ray's quarterback, "and the ball popped in the air. I just happened to be there and gathered it in. I caught it before it hit the ground. I already had one knee on the ground."

Two plays later, Carpenter burst over left tackle, broke free from Ray's nine-man line, and raced ninety-four yards for a touchdown.

"It was a straight hand-off, although I think Hubert Jordan and Boyd King cross-blocked on the play," Carpenter said. "They were in an eight-man front, pressing the line, trying to force us to punt. When I broke through the line, there wasn't a linebacker, so it was pretty open. The safety hit me on the right side, but I bounced off of him and it was a straight shot for the goal line."

Carpenter scored the other touchdown when he dashed sixty-two yards to the end zone in the third quarter. "It was a sweep, and everybody got blocked," said Carpenter, who also intercepted two passes.

Glynn Gregory (21) carries for a long gain in the 1956 state championship game against Corpus Christi Ray. (Photo courtesy of Flashlight)

Carpenter's 227 yards rushing, two touchdowns, and two interceptions remain one of the greatest performances in Texas high school state championship game history.

Gervis Galbraith, filling in for Stephens, was zero for two passing. The Eagles had failed to complete a pass in the final three weeks of the playoffs, but still won their third straight state championship. Galbraith's cousin, Gerald Galbraith, was the defensive star of the game, with the fumble recovery on the key first-quarter goal-line stand and a pass interception in the third quarter.

Abilene's defense was so dominating in the second half that the Eagles held Corpus Christi Ray to only one first down (on a penalty) and just twenty-nine yards rushing and none passing in the final two periods.

"I think the 1955 team was the best offensive team, but 1956 was the best defensive team," Rose said. "Other teams weren't as sophisticated as we were defensively. We always rotated to the strong side. Gregory and Carpenter were so good. We had two defensive backs who could run ten-flat or better. Midland was the only team that scored on a pass against us all year."

Moser agreed, calling the 1956 team his best defensive squad. "Since Gregory and Carpenter have been playing safety," Moser said, "there has never been a run made against us for over twenty yards, and there's never been a pass completed over our heads."

The 1956 team held its opposition to only 62 points while scoring 491. The Eagles scored forty or more points in each of nine games and held leads of at least thirty points at halftime nine times during the season.

Chuck Moser was the toast of Abilene as the architect of three consecutive state championship teams and a thirty-seven-game winning streak. He was more than just a football coach, however. A few weeks after Abilene's win over Corpus Christi Ray, Moser was installed as president of the Abilene Kiwanis Club.

The accolades rolled in for Moser and the Eagles at the conclusion of the 1956 season. The Texas Sports Writers Association named Moser the state's top football coach and Blacky Blackburn as the top high school baseball coach in the state at its banquet on January 4, 1957, in Dallas.

Glynn Gregory was also selected the high school football player of the year by the state's sports writers. Gregory ran for 1,142 yards, caught 19 passes for 553 yards, passed for 82 yards, scored 22 touchdowns, and kicked 56 extra points during his remarkable senior season. He booted 122 points after touchdown during the Eagles' three-year winning streak. That same day, Bobby Morrow was named Sportsman of the Year by *Sports Illustrated* magazine. It was quite a time to be a sports fan in Abilene.

Meanwhile, at nearby Stamford, Gordon Wood's team had completed its second straight unbeaten season and won its second straight Class AA state championship. Wood was 72-4 in six seasons.

Four Eagles were named to the Class AAAA all-state team. First-team honors went to tackle Rufus King, guard Stuart Peake and backs Glynn Gregory (the only unanimous selection) and Jimmy Carpenter. Guy Wells at guard and Jim Rose at center were named honorable mention all-state.

Peake, Wells, Gregory, Carpenter, Rufus King, and Hubert Jordan earned their third varsity letters. Nine members of the 1956 team were also members of the school's National Honor Society.

Abilene fans had one concern as they looked ahead to 1957: Would they be able to keep their football coach? Moser had plenty of opportunity to leave. He was one of four finalists for the head coaching position at the University of Missouri. The Tigers were seeking a replacement for Don Faurot, Moser's old coach, and his alma mater sought out the hottest high school coach in Texas. Moser, San Francisco 49ers assistant Phil Bengston, Michigan backfield coach Don Robinson, and Georgia Tech backfield coach Frank Broyles interviewed for the vacancy.

Moser told the *Reporter-News* that he thought Faurot was ready to offer him the job. But Moser withdrew his name. "I rode into St. Louis (site of the NCAA coaches convention) with Don (Faurot), and I just told him that I thought Frank would do a better job. I like Texas and Texas has been good to me. I just didn't think it would be best to go out of state to take a coaching job."

Broyles landed the job, and a couple of years later left Missouri for the head coaching job at the University of Arkansas, where he has remained as athletic director.

Moser's success in Abilene was drawing national attention. Not only was he a finalist for the Missouri job but he was also invited to be a guest lecturer at the NCAA coaches convention in St. Louis. His lecture on building a high school football program drew a standing-room-only crowd and the attention of the *St. Louis Post-Dispatch* newspaper, whose headline on a story about Moser read "The Abilene Story Amazes Prep Football Coaches."

Back in Abilene, the Eagle Booster Club gave the Abilene coaching staff $9,000 in cash and gift certificates at the annual football banquet. Moser was presented a check for $3,000.

Two years earlier, after the first state championship, Moser had been given a new car. "Chuck's car is two years old now," Eagle Booster Club president Stanley Smith told the gathering at Hardin-Simmons' Rose Field House, "and he's afraid to go very far from Abilene in it. We want to keep him that way."

Texas Western head coach Mike Brumbelow was the guest speaker at the banquet, but another college coach was also in attendance. Newly-named University of Texas coach Darrell Royal attended the banquet, hoping to recruit some of the talented Eagles. He landed

Peake and Rose, but others went to Oklahoma, SMU, Rice, and Hardin-Simmons. Six players on that 1956 team started as sophomores in college (freshmen weren't eligible in those days) and three others lettered as sophomores.

But the star of the banquet was Moser, who had announced he was staying in Abilene, hoping to stretch a record thirty-seven-game winning streak and capture an unprecedented fourth consecutive state championship.

CHAPTER 8

1957: Almost Another One

Riding the wave of a thirty-seven-game winning streak and three consecutive state championships, Abilene voters passed a $750,000 bond election to build a new football stadium in the spring of 1957. The Eagles had the most respected high school football program in the state, and a new stadium was needed to hold the crowds.

But surely Abilene couldn't keep its winning streak going. The Warbirds returned only one starter—linebacker Gerald Galbraith—and just eleven lettermen from the previous year's state championship squad as they prepared for their 1957 season opener against San Antonio Jefferson.

The experts didn't think Abilene could maintain its streak. "I was in Corpus Christi with my mom and daddy on vacation, running in the surf and getting ready for the season when it came out in the paper that we were picked to finish third in district," said Ronnie Ingle, a starting defensive end on the 1957 team. "I was a mad son-of-a-gun."

Gervis Galbraith, who had started in the playoffs the previous season in place of injured quarterback Harold Stephens, returned to direct the Eagles' offense. His cousin, Gerald Galbraith, who started on defense, took over as the starting center. Chuck Colvin and Bill Sides had both played a lot at halfback and fullback, respectively, a year earlier, but the rest of the Eagles' lineup was new.

Jimmy Perry and Mike McKinnis were named starting ends for the season opener. Mike Bryant and Ronnie Alldredge started at tackle, John Young and Truman Bridges at guard, the two Galbraiths at center and quarterback, Colvin and Stanley Cozby at halfbacks, and Sides at fullback.

Headlines in the first week of September in 1957 were dominated by the crisis at Little Rock Central High School. Arkansas Gov. Orval Faubus, defying an order from the federal government to integrate Little Rock schools, ordered Arkansas National Guardsmen on duty to keep black students from entering Central High School.

NEW SET OF STARS

The season opener against San Antonio Jefferson came on Friday, September 13, but *Reporter-News* sports writer Jimmy Browder noted that "the Friday the 13th jinx wilted before the more powerful hex of Coach Chuck Moser's orange shirt." Colvin, Cozby, and Sides scored touchdowns as Abilene High grabbed a 26-0 lead before Jefferson finally got on the board with a pair of touchdowns in the fourth quarter, making the final score 26-13.

Gregory, Carpenter, Caudle, and the other stars of the previous three championship seasons may have graduated, but it appeared that Abilene wouldn't miss a beat. A new set of stars had been waiting for the opportunity to shine on the varsity level in the state's best high school football program.

One of those was Colvin, who had a big game the next week in Abilene's 34-13 victory over Sweetwater, as noted by Oliver in the local paper: "Right halfback Chuck Colvin high-stepped his way to 192 yards and four touchdowns Friday night to lead Abilene to a hard-fought 34-13 victory over an aroused band of Sweetwater Mustangs and run the Warbirds' victory skein to 39 straight. However, the Mustangs gave the defending Class AAAA state champions all the football they wanted for three quarters before wilting to superior talent in the fine game played before an overflow crowd of 12,000 fans."

The previous season Gervis Galbraith had to step in at quarterback in the playoffs and the Eagles virtually abandoned their passing game. Galbraith, now a senior, made a couple of key passes to help Abilene stretch its one-touchdown advantage over Sweetwater. He hit Jimmy Perry with a thirty-five-yard pass. Then, after a loss and a clipping penalty, Galbraith threw a thirty-three-yard TD pass to Tim Walter to put the Eagles ahead 27-13.

Colvin had seventeen carries for 192 yards rushing and two touchdowns. Sides ran for 107 yards on twenty-four carries, and Cozby gained forty-two yards on nine attempts.

Headlines in the papers the two days leading up to Abilene's next game with Lubbock Monterey read "Citizens Watch Federal Troops Enter Little Rock" and "Paratroopers Escort 9 Negro Pupils to Classes" as President Eisenhower ordered integration of Little Rock Central.

The Monterey Plainsmen were no match for the Eagles, who were starting to put up numbers like the 1955 and 1956 teams. Abilene had twenty-seven first downs to four for Monterey in a 58-0 white-wash. Abilene amassed 400 yards total offense to just sixty-seven for Monterey as the Eagles' win streak reached forty.

There were plenty of offensive stars for Abilene. Sides rushed for 118 yards, Cozby scored three touchdowns, backup quarterback Freddie Martinez threw TD passes to Walter and Bob Swafford, and Colvin returned a punt sixty yards for another score.

AN OLD NEMESIS

Next on Abilene's schedule was a date with Breckenridge, the last team to have beaten the Eagles, three years earlier. Some were saying that this Breckenridge team was even better than the 1954 squad. But with three of its starting four in the backfield in 1954 now playing at the University of Oklahoma, that might be a little hard to imagine.

Still, Breckenridge was playing well. The Buckaroos were 2-0-1 after tying Sweetwater to open the season, then pulling off an upset of Wichita Falls and shutting out Gainesville.

The headline in the paper on game day read "First Artificial Moon Launched by Russians."

Jimmy Browder, in his game story the next day in the local paper, didn't use any Sputnik references, however. Instead, he compared the Eagles' offense to something West Texans know a lot more about as he described Abilene's 41-20 victory over Breckenridge:

"The Abilene Eagles struck with the quickness and deadliness of a rattlesnake—scoring two touchdowns in three plays—but the venom failed to halt the surging Breckenridge Buckaroos until the final gun sound Friday night with the Eagles in front 41-20. It was a blockbusting battle from start to finish as the Warbirds scored their 41st consecutive victory before a standing-room-only crowd of more than 9,000 at Breckenridge's Buckaroo Stadium."

Abilene scored on the second play of the game on Colvin's eighty-two-yard run. After Breckenridge went three and out and was forced to punt, Gervis Galbraith hit Cozby on a fifty-nine-yard pass and an Eagle touchdown. Only three minutes and fifty-five seconds had elapsed, but Abilene already owned a 13-0 lead.

Breckenridge, however, rallied to tie the game, 13-13, with 2:15 left in the second quarter. Less than a minute before halftime, Martinez hit Swafford with a thirty-five-yard TD pass, giving the Eagles' a 20-13 lead at intermission.

Sides scored three touchdowns on runs of three, ten, and two yards in the second half as Abilene pulled away for the victory.

About the only thing that could push high school and college football out of the top spot in the sports pages in the 1950s was the World Series. Baseball was the dominant pro sport back then, and the World Series was the premier sports event. On the day before Abilene faced Lubbock High, Lew Burdette threw a seven-hit shutout as the Milwaukee Braves blanked the New York Yankees 5-0 in game seven of the World Series. Burdette wasn't even scheduled to pitch, but teammate Warren Spahn had the flu, so Burdette picked up his third win and second shutout of the Series, the first pitcher since Christy Mathewson in 1905 to throw two shutouts in a World Series.

The next night, Abilene pitched a shutout of its own. Mal Elliott covered the game for the Abilene paper: "Coach Chuck Moser's

Abilene Eagles were awesome in their march toward the state high school consecutive victory record, registering No. 42 at the expense of an outgunned Tom S. Lubbock team, 39-0.

"The Warbirds used six different backs to score six touchdowns while employing three full teams. It was a lopsided affair after a 6-0 first quarter. The defending state AAAA champs rolled up almost 500 yards in total offense, 399 on the ground and 93 in the air, chalked up 26 first downs to four for Lubbock and held the Westerners to 83 rushing yards and four yards via the air lanes."

TYING AND BREAKING THE RECORD

The win over Lubbock High set the stage for a showdown with Waco. A victory over the Tigers would give the Eagles forty-three straight wins and a tie of the state record set by Hull-Daisetta, a small consolidated school near Beaumont in Southeast Texas, nearly twenty years earlier.

On October 14, however, heavy rains—as much as eleven inches in some areas—fell across much of Texas. As is often the case, Abilene received less than everyone else, just 2.85 inches officially. But areas around Ballinger, Cross Plains, and Eastland were flooding. The practice field at Waco flooded, too, forcing the Tigers to work out in the gym in preparation for the showdown with Abilene.

Whether that had any impact on the game, Waco was no match for the Eagles, who won, 27-7.

Another victory would give Abilene sole possession of the state record. The next Friday night, the Eagles opened district play with a 32-0 win over Big Spring for their forty-fourth consecutive win.

Browder wrote: "The Warbirds completely dominated the game and punched through the Steer defense for a total of 457 yards, 345 of it on the ground. Big Spring could muster its strength only long enough for one drive, and it fizzled on the Eagle 13 early in the second half."

Colvin and Cozby, who had moved to fullback to fill in for the injured Sides, each rushed for more than 100 yards in the victory.

Colvin, who had 108 yards rushing and two touchdowns, also caught four passes for eighty-three yards.

Bill Stages, the coach of the Corpus Christi Ray team that lost to Abilene in the 1956 state championship game, had been coach at Hull-Daisetta when it set the previous state record for consecutive victories. After Abilene broke the record, Stages told Oliver and the *Reporter-News* that he had been pulling for Moser and the Eagles to break his record.

"You hate to see something of long standing like that broken," Stages said. "After all, it lasted for 20 years, but you always are looking for new accomplishments in sports as well as everything else, and breaking records goes with it. It's just proof of the professional consistency of those Eagles. Tell the boys and Chuck they've got my heartiest congratulations."

Stages called Abilene's 1956 team the best high school football team he had ever seen. He also said Abilene had the most mobile defensive pursuit he had seen, and the Eagles' halfback-oriented offense had great balance.

Abilene had an open date on November 1, which was fortunate, because a flu epidemic hit the team. Moser said seventeen players had the flu and would have probably missed the game if the Eagles had to play. Several area schools closed because of the flu outbreak.

Moser worried about how the flu would impact his team as it prepared for a tough game with Odessa. Sports writer Mal Elliott wrote that the Eagles didn't miss a beat in a 19-0 shutout of the Bronchos: "The Eagles' offensive machinery was as sharp as ever as they boosted the state all-time consecutive victory record to 45 straight games, but they had to halt three serious Broncho scoring threats, two of them coming in the second half when the Red Hosses of Coach Hayden Fry came back strong."

Abilene scored on the game's opening possession on Colvin's two-yard run. Odessa countered with an impressive drive before the Eagles halted the Bronchos at the six-yard line. Joe Ward had the key stop for Abilene. The Eagles then drove ninety-six yards in eleven plays, scoring on a thirteen-yard run by Sides. Abilene also scored on its next possession on a short run by Colvin, but that was it for the scoring.

The Eagles posted their third straight shutout with a 41-0 victory over Midland, clinching another district championship. Abilene's defense didn't allow Midland a first down until the second quarter and didn't allow the Bulldogs to penetrate the twenty-yard line. John Young, Ronnie Ingle, Dale Graham, Don Hughes, Bob Swafford, Frank Aycock, Charles Harrison, Charles Lacy, and Alan Peake were credited with leading the defense.

Next up was the regular-season finale with San Angelo, a game that had traditionally been played on Thanksgiving Day. The game in 1957 fell on the Friday night before Thanksgiving, however, and it was a miserably cold night in San Angelo. The two teams combined for eighteen fumbles, with Abilene losing six of its twelve fumbles.

But, as Oliver chronicled in the paper, the Eagles still prevailed with a tight 12-6 win: "A sparse and frozen crowd of only 3,500 sat through the sub-freezing weather to watch the final district contest for the two old rivals. Snow, which fell here most of the day, covered most of the field and the places that weren't white were mushy mud where the gladiators had churned up the frozen stuff."

Cold weather and fumbles notwithstanding, the Eagles had completed the regular season unbeaten again, winning a fourth straight district title and running their winning streak to forty-seven. They were poised to make a run at an unprecedented fourth consecutive state championship.

Abilene opened the playoffs with a Thanksgiving Day game in El Paso. Oliver wrote it was a typical meeting with an El Paso opponent:

"Striking for 27 points in the first period, the Abilene Eagles continued their mastery over El Paso district champions here Thursday afternoon with a lopsided 60-0 verdict over the Austin High Panthers.

"The victory was the 48th straight for the three-time state champions and moved them into the quarterfinals of the 1957 Class AAAA playoffs against the winner of Friday night's Amarillo-Fort Worth Paschal game."

Seven different players scored in the victory over El Paso Austin. The Eagles scored on their first three possessions and built their lead to 41-0 by halftime. The reserves played the second half.

"I had a big ol' guy lined up against me," Ronnie Ingle said. "Wally Bullington told me before the game that if I'd whip him the first five minutes, I'd whip him all game. That's what I concentrated on." Ingle, however, never really got to find out if Bullington was right. The Eagles had their subs in the game by the second quarter.

NUMBER ONE VS. NUMBER TWO

It's hard to imagine that a team riding a forty-eight-game winning streak would be an underdog in a game, but that's exactly the situation the Eagles found themselves in as they prepared to face Amarillo in the state quarterfinals.

"It was the Game of the Century in Texas," Ingle said. "They were number one and we were number two. It was a real shootout."

The last time Abilene and Amarillo had met in the quarterfinals was 1936 when Amarillo beat the Eagles, 46-13. That Abilene team included running back John Kimbrough, who three years later led Texas A&M to its only national championship.

Oliver said the Sandies reminded him of Abilene's 1956 state championship team, featuring quarterback Soapy Sudbury, a pair of speedy halfbacks and "a big, rugged line anchored by guard Billy White, whom Amarillo coaches say is better than Stuart Peake." Many of the Amarillo players, including White and running back David Russell, went on to become college football standouts at Texas, Oklahoma, SMU, and New Mexico State.

Legendary *Amarillo Globe-News* sports editor Putt Powell claimed the 1957 Sandies were the best team in Amarillo history. That's saying something since Blair Cherry's Amarillo teams won three consecutive state football championships in 1934-36. Powell said the Sandies had not been tested all year, posting five shutouts and not allowing a single opponent to score more than one touch-down against them.

Amarillo beat Fort Worth Paschal, 26-6, a week earlier in bi-district, but Paschal was the first team to hold the Sandies under thirty-two points.

"Amarillo ran the split-T better than any team I'd seen in high school," Moser told long-time *Houston Chronicle* sports writer Bill McMurray in his 1985 book *Texas High School Football*. "Sudbury was a slick quarterback and ran the belly-option as good as anybody back then."

Amarillo was bigger and more experienced at every position. In fact, every Amarillo starter was at least a two-year letterman.

The hype was so big for this game that Oliver, writing in the Abilene paper, called the game "the Kentucky Derby, the Rose Bowl, the Olympics and the Davis Cup tournament all rolled into one."

Adding to the intrigue of the match-up was the fact that Joe Kerbel, who had been the coach at Breckenridge when the Buckaroos handed Abilene its last loss in 1954, was now coaching at Amarillo.

After winning back-to-back Class AA state championships in 1955 and 1956, Gordon Wood's Stamford team failed to make the playoffs in 1957 despite an 8-2 record. So Wood said he came to Abilene every day during the playoffs to watch the Eagles work out.

"One day I was at Abilene High's practice," Wood said, "and a junior varsity player told me, 'We're going to beat Amarillo.' I asked him how, since Amarillo had such a great team."

"I don't know how," the young Eagle told Wood, "but Coach Moser will figure out a way."

Indeed, Moser did figure out a way as Abilene upset Amarillo, 33-14. It may have been the most impressive victory in the Eagles' 49-game winning streak. Long-time Abilene football fans called the 1955 win over Tyler and the upset of Amarillo as the closest things to a perfect game ever played by the Eagles.

Moser credited his "Mud" defense that he had installed for that game as a key to the defense. He called it his "Mud" defense because he was afraid to run it except in bad weather. Many football teams, however, use the "Mud" defense strategy today. It's called a safety blitz.

"We were playing a 4-3 with four defensive backs and just before the ball was snapped, the safety away from the sideline would come up to the line of scrimmage and crash," Moser said. "His only job was to stop the quarterback. The end away from the sideline would then cover wide, contain, and the cornerbacks would sit back and wait for the flat pass. The other safety had coverage deep. Our safeties were tall, fast and tough, tremendous high school athletes."

Moser, who said the Eagles had spent three weeks preparing their "Mud" defense for Amarillo, called it a gamble because if the Sandies had sent two men deep on passes, the Eagles could not have stopped them with their "Mud" defense.

But the gamble paid off.

"That had to be one of our biggest wins," Moser said, "On paper, there was no way we should have defeated Amarillo."

Oliver, covering the game in the *Reporter-News*, said 4,600 Abilene fans made the trip to Amarillo and they saw an amazing performance: "There have been greater high school football teams in the history of Texas Interscholastic League football, but never one more determined than the Abilene Eagles of 1957 were Saturday afternoon.

"Coach Chuck Moser's magnificent charges spotted the No. 1-ranked Amarillo Sandies a first-quarter 7-0 lead, struck back to tie the count at 14-14 in the second quarter and then swept the Amarillo club by the wayside with a tremendous second-half attack for a 33-14 victory that boosted Abilene's winning streak to 49 straight."

"I really don't know if Moser really thought we could beat Amarillo," Ingle said. "When we were tied 14-14 at halftime, I'd never seen Coach Moser get that excited. But at halftime I think he saw the light at the end of the tunnel, that we really could beat them."

The big play of the game came in the fourth quarter and the Eagles leading 20-14. Abilene faced fourth down and nine yards to go for a first down at the Amarillo forty. The Eagles snapped the ball to Colvin, who was the up-back in Abilene's punt formation. Colvin ran fourteen yards for a first down. On the next play, Colvin raced twenty-six yards on a trap play to give Abilene a 26-14 lead. Cozby then scored the final touchdown with three minutes left.

"They had eight to twelve Division I players," Bullington said of Amarillo. "They were a super team. And, really, we weren't that strong. We ended that game right in front of a sandstorm."

Ingle said a sandstorm hit almost simultaneously with the final gun. He said it was raining mud on the Eagles as they celebrated their upset victory over Amarillo.

"Chuck always had about six junk plays that the other coach had never seen," Bullington said. "We put in a fake punt. On a crucial fourth down, we snapped it to the upback, Chuck Colvin, who ran for a first down. That nearly killed Joe Kerbel (the Amarillo coach). Really, they had a superior team."

Martinez had a big game as the Eagles' backup quarterback. He was four of seven passing for 106 yards, including a sixty-one-yard TD pass to Perry for Abilene's second score. Martinez also scored on a forty-five-yard run after receiving a lateral from Sides.

"I'll tell you the truth, I didn't think you could do it," Moser told his team in the locker room after the game. "I've never been prouder of any kids in my life. You guys played a real football game, I'll tell you."

Fort Worth Paschal coach Bill Allen, a twenty-year coaching veteran, told Oliver he'd never seen anything like the Eagles' performance against Amarillo.

"You line those two ball clubs up on the field," Allen said, "and personnel-wise, there isn't an Abilene player, maybe with the exception of fullback Bill Sides, who could make that Amarillo starting lineup. But, look at that score. That ball club is a tribute to the greatest coach in the history of Texas high school football and to that terrific desire that he instills in those boys."

Amazingly, the Amarillo game marked the first time in Abilene's forty-nine-game winning streak that the Eagles had been behind in a game. Moser also noted that the fake punt was the first time the Eagles had run that play since Bobby Jack Oliver ran with it against Lubbock in 1953.

THE STREAK ENDS

The euphoria of the upset win over Amarillo didn't last long, however. A week later, Highland Park stunned Abilene, rallying for a 20-20 tie in the Class AAAA semifinals at the Cotton Bowl. The Scots advanced to the state championship game because they had more penetrations inside the twenty-yard line, a method that was used to break ties in high school football games in Texas back then.

"I didn't know anything about penetrations or first downs," Ingle said. "I was ready to keep playing."

It took more than thirty years before that rule was finally changed. Teams play overtime now if a game ends in a tie at the conclusion of regulation play.

"I don't think we took Highland Park lightly," Ingle said. "The Amarillo game just took so much out of us."

Even Moser admitted afterwards that he thought the winner of the Abilene-Amarillo game would have a tough time against Highland Park because the two teams had been so high for that game that there was bound to be an obvious letdown.

The *Abilene Reporter-News* headline across the top of the front page the next day simply read: "End of the Road."

That said it all. In the sports section, Oliver told the story of the stunning tie/loss that ended the Eagles' remarkable forty-nine-game winning streak:

"The Highland Park Scotties turned the Cotton Bowl into a mammoth tomb for the Abilene Eagles here Saturday afternoon as 30,000 stunned fans looked on in disbelief.

"The Scotties, two touchdown underdogs, connected on a lightning-strike 58-yard desperation pass with only 3:36 left in the game to tie the count at 20-20 in the Class AAAA playoff semifinals, and gained the right to meet Port Arthur next week on penetrations, 5-3.

"Thus for the first time in four years, the Eagles won't be playing for the state championship, and although their 50-game undefeated streak remained intact, their national record of 49 consecutive victories was broken."

Abilene had trailed 7-6 and 14-13, but the Eagles took the lead when Martinez and Cozby hooked up on a seventy-six-yard touchdown pass with six seconds remaining in the third quarter to give the Eagles a 20-14 advantage.

The winning play for Highland Park came on a third down late in the fourth quarter. The Scots needed nine yards for a first down when Bob Reed hit speedster Jack Collins, who turned it into a fifty-eight-yard scoring play to tie the game 20-20. Collins made the extra point, but the Scots were penalized for illegal motion. He missed on the second attempt, but Highland Park still won on penetrations.

Three years later, Jack Collins, then a University of Texas running back, was pictured on the cover of a new magazine that has become almost as much of a tradition in Texas as football itself. Collins was the cover boy for the first *Dave Campbell's Texas Football* magazine.

In 1957, he was the key player in the biggest story in high school football. Collins gave his coach, Tugboat Jones, the victory he had been looking for since 1953 when he was the coach at Midland High. Jones had some great teams, led by fullback Wahoo McDaniel, but the Bulldogs had never been able to beat Moser's Abilene Warbirds.

Jones, an Abilene Christian College graduate and brother-in-law of former ACC coach Garvin Beauchamp, said he never had enough speed at Midland to beat Abilene. When he took the Highland Park job in the spring of 1956, he made no bones about the fact that his goal at Highland Park was to beat Abilene.

"That's what I came here for, to beat Abilene," he told his team that spring. "I left Midland because we didn't have enough good boys to beat Abilene. I think you are the ones who can do the job."

Thanks to Collins' blazing speed, Jones accomplished his goal.

"That was the most devastating thing," said John Young, who later had a lengthy coaching career in the National Football League with the Houston Oilers and New Orleans Saints. "The scar still hasn't healed. I thought losing was something that happened to other teams. They didn't beat us, but they stopped us from going on. We truly believed that the only way someone would score on us was if we made mistakes, and we made too many mistakes that day. We felt like we let our little world down."

The 1957 season had ended a week early for the Eagles, who finished with a 12-0-1 record after outscoring their opponents 442-93. Colvin led Abilene in rushing with 1,325 yards on 184 carries and 17 touchdowns and also caught 12 passes for 225 yards. Sides rushed for 1,029 yards and Cozby gained 557 yards on the ground.

The forty-nine-game winning streak was also over, but the numbers that Moser's Eagles compiled during the remarkable four-year run were mind-boggling:

- Abilene scored 1,774 points during the winning streak, an average of 35.1 per game, while allowing only 311 points, an average of just 6.3 points per contest.
- The Eagles allowed no runs longer than fifteen yards in thirty-seven of the forty-nine games and had no touchdown passes thrown on them in thirty-three games.
- In thirty-six of the forty-nine games, Abilene held a lead of at least twenty points at halftime.

The newspaper account of the Highland Park game didn't mention the fact, but two starters didn't play in that game for Abilene.

"We gave those slips, and we had two players who were not passing three subjects before that game, so they did not play," Moser recalled years later. "We passed that slip around every week, and if you weren't passing three subjects, you weren't going to play that week." Even in the biggest game of the year, Moser's self-imposed no-pass, no-play rules were in effect.

Did anyone try to talk Moser into changing his rules and allowing the two players to play?

"We knew better than that," Bullington said.

Former players interviewed don't even remember what players were forced to miss the game. They just remember that the eligibility slips were a critical part of being an Abilene Eagle, and they never questioned the rule.

"I don't recall it happening before, but it probably did, although not starters," said Gerald Galbraith, who was injured and didn't play in the game against Highland Park. "The two didn't play because of a coach-imposed rule. The important thing is the rule was the rule. It wasn't bent or broke to satisfy the time."

Galbraith remembers the quiet bus ride home, punctuated by a rousing reception from Abilene fans.

"Cars were lined up in the Elmdale area, east of town," he said. "They had their lights on and were honking, following the bus back into town. That was probably the biggest homecoming we had ever had. Talk about support. That was the epitome of the support we had in those days."

The next morning, as the realization of the first loss in more than three years settled in on Abilene football fans, Moser was at his usual place—teaching his junior high boys Sunday school class at St. Paul Methodist Church. His lesson that day was "Everything Happens for the Best." It was a lesson he had had planned for several years— when and if the Eagles finally lost a football game.

He told the thirty-two youngsters and other visitors crammed into the room that morning that the loss to Highland Park "will help us have a better team next year. It will make us appreciate winning more."

Moser also said that "now we know how those forty-nine teams that we beat have felt."

CHAPTER 9

The Coach and the Quarterbacks

David Bourland may have had the most unique perspective of Moser's coaching philosophy of any of the five quarterbacks who guided the Eagles during the winning streak. By chance, Bourland ended up playing under Moser for four years. He was a ninth grader in the spring of 1953 when Moser arrived in Abilene for his first spring practice.

Don Harber, who became Moser's first starting quarterback that fall, missed spring workouts with a broken arm. His backup, Glen Belew, who later was moved to safety, had the chickenpox. Bourland had been the starting quarterback that fall at North Junior High, while Carlton Winkles was the starting quarterback at South Junior High. Winkles' father died, however, and Winkles had to quit football and get a job to help support his family.

That left Bourland as the only quarterback that spring.

"I think Coach Moser was ready to go back to Corpus Christi," Bourland said. "I switched jerseys and played quarterback for both sides in the annual ice cream game (the intrasquad scrimmage held at the end of spring workouts). But that helped me."

Bourland had to wait his turn to become the Eagles' quarterback in the fall, playing third team as a sophomore and backing up H.P. Hawkins on the 1954 state championship team.

Hawkins said that was typical. Moser always carried a senior quarterback, a junior quarterback, and a sophomore quarterback on the varsity. The senior always started, but the others got to play.

"He had a standing rule, if you were twenty-eight points ahead the first team doesn't play," said Hawkins. "He was building all the time. I think that was part of his success. When the game was in hand, the running backs and quarterbacks came out. He started developing kids when the lead was in the comfortable margin, and there were many games when we had a comfortable lead."

Hawkins and Harber both went on to play quarterback at Abilene Christian College. Harold "Hayseed" Stephens, the quarterback of the 1956 state championship team, was quarterback at Hardin-Simmons and then played for his old college coach Sammy Baugh and the New York Titans in the American Football League.

Harber lives in Graham. Hawkins is coaching in Hereford on former Abilene High assistant Don Delozer's staff. Bourland, who played football briefly at Texas Tech, sells real estate in Abilene. Stephens, who found success in the oil business as well as his work as an evangelist, died in the fall of 2003. Gervis Galbraith, who became a surgeon, and Freddie Martinez live in Abilene.

Everyone agrees that one of the secrets to Moser's success was his attention to detail in scouting and preparation. Never was that more evident than in his development of quarterbacks.

"Every morning before school, we would have a twenty-minute meeting," Bourland said. "At noon, we'd have another twenty-minute group meeting, and then we'd meet at the stadium before practice. If you were late to a meeting, you had to run ten 100-yard sprints after practice."

The impression that Moser made on his team to be on time was never more evident than one day when Bourland's car was involved in an accident.

"Most of us used to go home for lunch," Bourland said. "When the bell rang, we'd tear out for our cars because we had only thirty minutes to get home, eat lunch and be back at school in time for our meeting."

On this particular day, Bourland raced to his car, which was parked on the side street beside Abilene High, only to discover that

H.P. Hawkins

Gervis Galbraith

Freddie Martinez

someone had taken the corner too wide as they came off South First Street and had collided with the side of his car.

"I quickly found my cousin, who usually rode home with me for lunch, and told her she'd have to make other arrangements for lunch," he said. "And then I ran to Coach Moser's office."

"I've got a problem," Bourland said to the coach, explaining that someone had hit his car.

"You do have a problem," Moser responded, "but don't be late for the meeting."

Bourland said he found a cafeteria worker who was a friend of his family and borrowed money for lunch, thus ensuring he made Moser's meeting on time.

Unlike today when coaches call the plays, Moser allowed his quarterbacks to call their own plays.

"He used to tell us if we get beat, you as the quarterback and I as the coach will be criticized," said Hawkins. "The game has really changed. At some point it evolved. I guess the pressure is greater on

David Bourland

Don Harber

Charles McCook

Harold "Hayseed" Stephens

high school coaches today. Turning their future over to seventeen-year-olds just doesn't happen anymore."

The Abilene quarterbacks may have called their own plays, but they were well prepared by Moser.

"We spent one evening a week at his home, starting in July or August," Hawkins said. "He'd grill us on Thursdays. The senior quarterback was in the hot seat. He'd give you time, down, distance, weather conditions, and situations, and then you'd call a play. His question was always why, and you better be able to explain why you called that particular play."

"One of the things he taught that sticks out is responsibility," Hawkins added. "We had a responsibility. We were him (Moser) on the field."

QUARTERBACK MATERIAL
(from Moser's *Abilene High School Football Organization* book)

1. Quarterback Material
In meetings with the quarterback, we believe these are some very important points for the quarterback to know. They should be explained and discussed frequently in the quarterback meetings.

2. Standard Defenses
The quarterback should be familiar with these defenses to the extent of knowing some of their strong and weak areas. The lines indicate areas where we think about throwing and the spots areas where we think of running.

3. Formations
The quarterback should have in mind the formations we have worked on in order to take advantage of weakness in defenses.

4. Pass Coverage Sheet
This will help the quarterback to determine the type of pass coverage that is being used by the opposing team and by going over these will help him to be more consistent in his passing game.

5. Blocking Situations
By going over this sheet in meetings with the quarterback, he will be able to direct the running game with more consistency. We want him to know where to try to hurt these situations quickly so as not to waste plays running.

6. Opponent Summary Sheet
This is a condensed report on the opponent for the coming game and should be studied each day by the quarterback. This sheet is compiled from the scouting form and is given to the quarterback early in the week to stress the main points of the scout report.

PUNTING
1. Always kick back of the fifty yard line on fourth down unless told differently.
2. Punt on first or second down back of the ten yard line, unless vs. the wind.
3. Punt when there is no chance of a first down.
4. Caution your line to block hard and get down fast; tell where you intend for the punter to kick. (Usually toward the open field)
5. Punt on short or long counts. (Usually silent count)
6. Think punt when you have the wind, hold ball against the wind.
7. Kick at the end of the quarter with the wind.

PASSING

1. Know when <u>not</u> to pass, as ahead 1 to 6 points, back of the 15 yard line, and on the goal line with short yardage.
2. When to pass - as when your opponents are not expecting.
   1st down
   2nd down and 1 or 2 yards to go
   When defensive backs are tight
   vs a 8 or 71 defense - short passes

THINGS TO ALWAYS KNOW AND THINK ABOUT

1. Down and yardage
2. Who made the last tackle
3. Score and time to play
4. Position on field (Sideline and yard line)

PLAYERS TO ASK ABOUT DEFENSE

1 and 2 hole - guards
3 and 4 hole - tackles
5 end 6 hole - ends
7 and 8 hole - half backs

RUNNING

1. Know the defense (Run on down if they shift just before the ball is snapped.)
2. Know your own personnel (Who and where to run when you need two yards.)
3. Know what plays are best vs certain defenses.
4. Do not use laterals, pitchouts, reverses, or ball handling plays back of the 15 yard line. (QB carry the ball more)
5. Run over linemen who drift or tackle out of position, or who are <u>standing up</u>.
6. If plan to change plays at the line go on hut.

GENERAL

1. Open up when behind (13 points)
2. Get information from substitutes.
3. Use scoring plays after recovery of fumble, block kick or intercepted pass. Have a play you know is set up.
4. Find a weak player and work on him.
5. Use the same play until they stop it. Then, you know how they stopped it.
6. Know plays—where they hit, when they will work best, and know the key blocking.
7. Speak clearly and with force in the huddle.
8. Do not criticize players, encourage them.
9. Always tell line to cover passes.
10. Have confidence in yourself and never give up.
11. Throw more quick passes with less number linebacker (as 7 or 8)

"On Mondays, he gave you the play book for that week, which had a scouting report of your next opponent," Bourland said. "On Tuesdays, you'd have a test. You had to memorize the name, number, weight, and position of all the starters. If you flunked the test, you moved to the second team."

In addition to the three team meetings held each day, Moser also met with his top three or four quarterbacks during third period each day.

"He'd give us a test every day," Bourland said. "He'd have these eight-by-ten cards of the ten basic defenses with X's and O's. You had to sit in front of him and he'd hold up the card for three seconds. He'd put it down and ask what defense that was. If there was a man over center, it was an odd front. Then you'd look and see if there was anyone over the guards and if the linebackers were off the line. The linemen had to be as smart as we did because we used rule blocking."

Rule blocking meant the linemen had rules to go by on every play, depending on what defense their opponents were in. Bourland said he still remembers the rule for the right guard on the "four-play," which was a dive play. "The right guard's rule on that play was on-in-out-linebacker. That meant if a guy was on him, he blocked him. If not, he'd block the guy inside him. If there wasn't anyone on him or inside him, he'd block the guy outside him. If none of those three happened, then he'd block the linebacker."

Bourland said the quarterbacks had the option of changing the play at the line of scrimmage. The quarterbacks would call three numbers. The first number would signify if he was going to change the play. The second number would be the new play, and the third number wouldn't mean anything, but that gave the linemen an extra second or two to remember what their rules were on the new play.

Sometimes, things didn't always work out like they were planned. "In the state championship game against Tyler, I called a trap to James Welch, our fullback," Bourland said. "When we got to the line of scrimmage, they were in a gap-eight defense, so I changed the play to a pitch out to Welch. Well, I guess it was my fault because I didn't turn around and make sure he heard me. When I turned to pitch out to him, Welch runs right into me. He hits me in the face. No one remembers those plays."

Hawkins said Moser only questioned him one time about his play call. "We were playing Amarillo my junior year. We had the ball on their forty, and it was fourth down. I called a thirty-two trap fake in the middle, and then I hit Bob Gay on a pass for a touchdown. When I came off the field, Moser asked me if I realized it was fourth down. I said yes, but I thought they'd be looking for a running play. All he wanted to know was if I knew it was fourth down and why I called what I did."

Bourland said Moser didn't want anyone except the quarterback to talk in the huddle. "But I told our guys if they could handle their man to tell me. We were playing Lubbock, and Sam (Caudle) told me he could beat his man. So I called two plays in a row to set up a play in which Caudle would block his man."

Moser, however, sent in a different play on third down. Bourland changed Moser's play and called his own. "When I came back to the bench, he chewed me out. I explained I had been setting up that play. He said, 'Well, we did make forty yards on it.'"

Moser was not as understanding of another one of Bourland's calls. "He had devised a trick play. I would fake a hand-off to the fullback on the belly series and then bring the ball around my back and switch hands. I called the play, and he jumped all over me. He said, 'Don't run a trick play without me sending it in.' I understood. He was saving it for the right situation."

Moser didn't miss a beat in thinking of every situation. For example, Bourland said Moser let the quarterback choose the game ball the team would use in the game. "He'd let you pick out the ball that felt best to you. He was way ahead of his time, and he never missed anything."

Moser not only demanded perfection from his team on the field and in the classroom, but he also expected them to act appropriately at all times.

"He expected you to be a gentleman off the field," Bourland said. "If you weren't, he didn't want you on his team. He'd get letters from hotels where we stayed, complimenting us on how well we behaved. He'd read those letters to us."

Bourland said Moser also warned the team about gamblers before their state championship game against Tyler.

"We were staying in Fort Worth, the night before the game," Bourland said. "I stepped out of the elevator, and this huge, fat man introduced himself to me. We started talking, and he asked how I felt about the game. Then he asked what we were going to run on the first play."

Bourland remembered what Moser had told him. "I don't mean any disrespect, sir, but our coach told us to tell anyone who asks if they want to know what we're going to run they'll have to buy a ticket tomorrow. He just laughed and shook all over."

All of the Abilene quarterbacks from 1954-57—Hawkins, Bourland, Stephens, Gregory, Galbraith, and Martinez—played an integral part in Abilene's forty-nine-game winning streak. They called the plays and were the leaders on the field, thanks to the training and confidence Moser gave them.

"I don't know any other teams that changed the play at the line of scrimmage or had rule blocking like we did," Bourland said. "Moser was way ahead of his time. He never missed anything."

CHAPTER 10

The All-Staters

Chuck Moser had fifteen players selected first-team all-state during his seven years as the head coach at Abilene High. Actually, fourteen different players, since Glynn Gregory was a two-time all-stater. Nearly fifty years later, these "best of the best" still remember their high school football careers fondly and give credit for their successes both on and off the field to Moser and his staff.

BOBBY JACK OLIVER
All-state tackle 1953

Bobby Jack Oliver only had the opportunity to play football for one season under Coach Moser, graduating the year before Abilene began its remarkable run of three consecutive state championships. But Oliver got to know Moser really well.

"He moved into a rent house on Willis Street behind my parents' house," Oliver said. "We lived on Ballinger Street. The Mosers had a TV but we didn't, so he'd invite me over on Wednesday nights to watch replays of Notre Dame football games. Doris would fix me hot chocolate. He'd say, 'Look at that line, how they're firing out.'"

Oliver said Coach Moser made football fun. "We laughed a lot, but he was serious, too. He was human, but, boy, did we respect him."

At 6-3, 225 pounds, Oliver was the biggest player Moser coached during his seven years in Abilene. But he had assistant coach Bob Groseclose to thank for even having Oliver on his team.

"I didn't like football in junior high," Oliver said. "If you're a lineman, you don't have any fun in practice. I didn't go out for spring practice between my ninth grade and tenth grade years. Coach Groseclose kept getting on me. He'd ask, 'How you going to go to college?

Your parents can't afford it. You're a big, strong kid. You need to be playing football.' About two weeks before the season started that fall, I went over the field house and told the coaches I was going out for football. I have to give credit to Coach Groseclose for talking me into playing football, and I'm sure glad he did."

Oliver was the only sophomore to make the varsity that season. By the time he was a senior, he was named all-state and received a scholarship to Baylor. He was

Bobby Jack Oliver

drafted in the third round by the Chicago Cardinals, but instead signed with Toronto in the Canadian Football League. He spent seven seasons in the CFL.

Oliver's wife, the former Betty Trentham, was a year ahead of Bobby Jack at Abilene High. The two married while he was at Baylor, and she was seriously injured in a car wreck near Slaton, as she was driving to California to see Bobby Jack play in the East-West Shrine game.

"She's had two hip replacements, but she's a trooper," Oliver said.

He has owned his own business, Oliver Sales Company in Richardson, since 1969. His company represents Os-Tech, a processing printed circuit board used in the chemical and electronic industry.

Although he played on the varsity all three years in high school, Oliver never played a full football season.

"I played in three games as a sophomore," he said. "Then my junior year, I dislocated my shoulder the first day of practice. My senior year, I did the same thing. I played in only eight games as both a junior and as a senior."

When he looks back on his football career, Oliver reflects about how close he came to a state championship at Abilene and a national championship at Baylor.

"We had a 14-0 lead on Odessa," he recalled. "They cut it to 14-12 and then a pass interference call—that the film showed later was a wrong call—kept a drive alive for them and they beat us 19-14."

Odessa won district and advanced to the state championship game, while Abilene, disheartened by the loss to the Bronchos, lost 7-6 to Pampa the next week before rolling over its opposition with four lopsided victories to end the 1953 season with a 7-2-1 record.

"The same scenario happened in 1956 at Baylor," he said. The Bears were unbeaten until a loss to Texas A&M. The Aggies' Jack Pardee fumbled and Baylor recovered, according to Oliver. The officials, however, ruled that Pardee was down, and the Aggies went on to score the winning touchdown. TCU then beat Baylor, 7-6, the next week.

Baylor won the rest of its games that season, including a win over Tennessee, led by halfback Johnny Majors, in the Sugar Bowl.

"I was at a reunion at Baylor recently, and we were talking about how close we came to winning a national championship," he said. The same could be said of the Oliver and the Eagles in their first season under Moser.

TWYMAN ASH
All-state end 1954

Twyman Ash was much more than a one-play wonder. He was an all-state selection as a senior in 1954 and a two-year starter for the Eagles in both football and basketball. But the 6-2, 170-pound Ash will always be remembered for one play, his finger-tip grab of the winning touchdown pass from H.P. Hawkins in the 1954 state championship.

Ash leaped up above defensive back David Webster of Houston Stephen F. Austin to make the catch at the five-yard line. He then turned and tumbled into the end zone, completing the twenty-nine-yard scoring play with fifty-six seconds to go to give Abilene a 14-7

Twyman Ash

victory over Austin and the Eagles' first of three consecutive state championships.

It wasn't the last matchup between Ash and Webster, however. "I went to Rice and he went to Texas," Ash recalled. "The next year we were playing the Longhorns in a freshman game. It was almost the same situation, and I caught the winning pass over the top of him in the end zone. He looked down at me and said, 'You're the luckiest son-of-a-bitch I know.'"

Ash may be the only former player of Moser's to be hired by Moser, too. When Ash graduated from Rice, he taught and coached for one year at Houston Jones. Moser, who by then had quit coaching and was the athletic director for the Abilene school district, hired Ash to come back to Abilene High as an assistant coach.

"He called me into his office the first day," Ash said, "and said you can't be a good coach unless you're a great teacher. You have to do lesson plans, just like the other teachers." Ash spent five years as an assistant to Wally Bullington at Abilene High.

"I don't think the coaches today have near the programs of caring if the kids do well off the field," Ash said.

He has a favorite story about Moser's ability to keep track of his players.

"My senior year, a friend of mine was dating a girl from Odessa. (after football season was over). He talked me into going to Odessa, and he'd have his girlfriend set me up with a date. I talked my dad into letting me take our car, so we drove to Odessa. We went on the date and then we spent the night at her folks' house. We had dinner on Sunday with her parents and then we drove back to Abilene. We didn't get back until about 4 o'clock Sunday afternoon.

"The next morning, I walked into school and a teacher gave me a note that Mr. Moser wanted to see me in his office. I went down there, and he said, 'I understand you had a date in Odessa Saturday night.' I said, 'Yes, sir.'

"He said, 'Why do you want to go to Odessa? We've got the best girls right here in Abilene.' He wrung me out. He said, 'I don't think you need to go out there,' and I never did again. He said these girls in Abilene are a lot nicer and sweeter.

"To this day, I don't know how he found out. But he was a real stickler about things. You couldn't let your girlfriend wear your new letter jacket."

Ash's mother had worked for Luby's Cafeteria. After coaching for five years in Abilene, Ash went to work in management for Luby's. He spent the rest of his career working for Luby's. He currently lives in Nederland.

JOHN THOMAS
All-state guard 1954

Ask most of the former Abilene players during the Moser era to name the team's "toughest" player and you'll get the same answer: John Thomas. Thomas was an all-state guard on the Eagles' 1954 state championship squad.

"Coach Watkins called John Thomas '178 pounds of dynamite with a two-inch fuse,'" said end Hollis Swafford, a teammate of Thomas' on the 1953 and 1954 teams. "He was a nose guard who would make tackles on end sweeps."

"John was exceptionally tough," said Bob Hubbard, a starting defensive end on the 1954 team who remains one of Thomas' closest friends today. "At one of our reunions, Coach Moser put his hand on

John's shoulder and said this is the best football player I coached. That raised a few eyebrows, but when John put on his uniform, his personality changed completely. He was a tough football player."

Thomas started at nose guard as a junior and then was the Eagles' starting nose guard on defense and guard on offense as a senior. He

John Thomas

was best known for his defensive play, making life miserable for the center lined up across from him.

"I'd just hit him across the chest with my forearm and go from there," Thomas said.

Thomas and Swafford both remember one particular drill that the Abilene linemen had to run. "In practice on pass plays, if a lineman's man got to the quarterback, he'd have to stand back there like the quarterback and hold the ball up in the air," Swafford said. "All the defensive linemen would hit you. It was tough."

Did Thomas ever have to do that? "Not too often," he said. "It made you want to hold your block."

After earning all-state honors at Abilene High, Thomas went to Allen Academy in Bryan, which was a prep school for Texas A&M. Thomas decided not to go to Texas A&M, however, instead coming back home to play football at McMurry College. He was named an all-American at McMurry and had a tryout with the Houston Oilers in 1962.

When he was released by the Oilers at the end of the exhibition season, Thomas played semi-pro football with the Jacksonville (Florida) Bears. He then returned to Texas, worked in the oil fields, ran a printing press for twenty years in Temple, and drove a truck until he retired. He and his wife still live in Temple.

Thomas called the loss to Breckenridge in 1954—the Eagles' last loss before beginning their forty-nine-game winning streak—a turning point for Abilene football. "After the Breckenridge game, everyone gelled. We played Midland and beat them good, but Breckenridge was the turning point. After that game, we changed our attitude."

Thomas said playing for Moser was one of the highlights of his career. "He was really a fabulous man to me. He knew how to teach it. He put the material out where you had no trouble knowing what you needed to do. He didn't put up with any nonsense. He knew how to get the best out of each boy. We had a lot of talent, but he was able to develop it."

JIMMY MILLERMAN
All-state running back 1954

Jim Millerman attended the Big 12 Conference track meet in Austin last year and struck up a conversation with another fan in the stands. The other person had played for El Paso against the Abilene Eagles in the 1950s.

"The thing I remember about those Abilene High teams is all the green grass the punt returners had," the El Paso native told Millerman, who was often the recipient of the Eagles' impressive blocking on punt returns.

"Teams feared our downfield blocking more than anything else," said Cullen Hunt, an honorable mention all-state tackle and a teammate of Millerman's on Abilene's 1954 championship team.

Millerman, who went on to run track and play football at Baylor, said he was fortunate to win two state championships in the same calendar year. As a junior in the spring of 1954, he ran on the Eagles' sprint relay team that won a gold medal at the state track meet and recorded the fastest time in the nation. The Eagles won the state team track championship. Then that fall, Millerman was an all-state running back for the state champion Abilene football team.

Millerman credits track coach Bob Groseclose for playing a role in his football success. "I ran a ten-flat 100 as a ninth-grader in junior high," Millerman said, "but don't ask about how strong a tailwind I had. Coach Groseclose came over to the city junior high track meet at

Fair Park. He told me I needed to do chin-ups because I needed to build my upper body strength. We didn't have weight-lifting back then.

"So I got a chinning bar in my garage, and I did chin-ups every night before I went to bed. I never got a shoulder hurt in all the years

Jimmy Millerman

I played football. Groseclose was interested in the smaller points, just like Moser."

Moser's attention to detail amazed Millerman.

"Years later, we were having lunch," he said, "and Coach Moser said, 'I knew you really wanted to play football.'" Millerman asked how.

"When I first came to Abilene, I got the school records of all the players," Moser said. "When you were in the third grade, they gave a test and asked what do you want to do when you grow up. You said you wanted to play football for the Abilene Eagles." Millerman couldn't believe Moser knew what he had written on a paper in the third grade.

"He got into your psyche," Millerman said. "That's what made him a great coach. He was always a step ahead of everyone else. He had special teams ten years before I heard of special teams. We had mimeographed sheets for everybody to study on Monday each week with a scouting report of our opponent. When I got to college, I found out everyone didn't do that. I got to see how advanced he was."

Millerman received his degree in insurance from Baylor and came back to Abilene to work for his father in Millerman & Millerman Insurance. Ten years later, he moved to Dallas to open a Millerman & Millerman Insurance office there. He has lived in Dallas ever since. He sold the Abilene and Dallas agencies to HRH Insurance about ten years ago, but he continues to work for HRH.

SAM CAUDLE
All-state guard 1955

An alert reaction by a junior high coach may have kept Abilene from having to forfeit several games in 1953.

Sam Caudle's family had moved from Spur to Abilene during the Christmas vacation his ninth-grade year. The next year, Caudle started out on the B team, but Moser decided to move the sophomore up to the varsity for the first district game. When one of the junior high coaches learned that, he pointed out to Moser that Caudle had moved to Abilene in the middle of the previous school year. In those days, transfer students had to sit out a full year before they were eligible to play varsity sports.

"I didn't know the rules," Caudle recalled. "Coach Moser called me in and asked when I had moved here. I told him at Christmas. He asked if I had played ninth grade football at Spur. I said yes. He said I wasn't eligible to play on the varsity that year. So I played the rest of my sophomore year on the junior varsity. It worked out well, though, because we had an undefeated B team."

Although he was small for a lineman at 5-9, 170 pounds, no one could keep Caudle out of the lineup the next two years. He started at guard and linebacker as both a junior and senior. In 1955, Caudle was not only named all-district and first team all-state but he was also named a high school all-American.

There wasn't a national letter-of-intent back then, just conference letters-of-intent. So Caudle signed with both Oklahoma and Southern Methodist University.

"I went to SMU because my girlfriend was going there," he said. Caudle married his high school sweetheart, Ruth Ann Polk.

Caudle's collegiate career encompassed the era of limited substitution in college football. He played on the alternate team as a sophomore and a senior at SMU. He missed his junior year after having knee surgery.

Caudle earned degrees in math and economics from SMU. After working for Republic Bank in Dallas for a year, he went into the investment business.

"I've been in the securities business in one form or another ever since," he said.

Ask Caudle, who still lives in Dallas, about individual performances, and you won't get many answers.

"I never thought individually," he said. "It was the whole team deal for me."

Sam Caudle

He called the win over Midland High to clinch the district title and the victory over Houston Stephen F. Austin for the state championship in 1954 as two of the highlights of his career.

"Our win over Tyler in the state championship game in 1955 was as good as we ever played," Caudle said. "The guy I played in front of, Byron Carruthers of Tyler, became a good friend of mine here in Dallas."

And what does Carruthers think about the Eagles' victory over Tyler in the 1955 title game? "He thinks we got lucky," Caudle said.

Caudle knows better, however. He says the difference was coaching. "Chuck Moser was the difference. We were just kids, like everyone else. But our coaches were so much better than our college coaches. Chuck was way ahead of his time, in planning and attention to detail. He was always consistent. We never questioned him because what he said usually worked. He paid tremendous attention to fundamentals. I don't know if we worked harder, but I know we worked smarter than other teams. Hank (Watkins) had a lot to do with that, too.

"Chuck made us better players. With my size, I wouldn't have been worth a damn if I didn't have good technique. You wanted to do good. You were afraid of Chuck, but you wanted to do good for him. He was real fair."

FRED GREEN
All-state end/linebacker/punter 1955

Freddie Green admits he sometimes wonders how life might have turned out differently.

Green, an all-state end/linebacker/punter on Abilene's 1955 state championship football team, was also a two-time all-state selection in baseball for the Eagles, who lost a controversial heartbreaker to Paris in the 1955 state tournament final and then won the first of two straight state championships in 1956.

Green had plenty of offers to play football in college but, instead, accepted a scholarship to play baseball at Southern Methodist University. That was not Green's most difficult decision, however. He also had to weigh an offer to sign a professional baseball contract with the Detroit Tigers.

"Baseball teams had something called a 'bonus baby' back then," Green said. "They could sign one player to a big bonus." The Tigers had offered Green a $35,000 bonus to sign with them.

"My grandfather and I were set to sign with the Tigers after the state championship game in Austin (in 1956)," he said, "but my grand-mother ruled the roost and she said no. She said I was going to college."

So Green signed with SMU. But he had knee surgery shortly before the start of base-ball season that next spring. "I had hurt my

Freddie Green

knee in the Breckenridge game my senior year," he said. "I played the rest of the season with my cartilage torn up. I taped it up like a brace every day. As a punter, that's difficult."

Because he had to miss so many classes after having knee surgery, Green was placed on academic probation at SMU and was going to be ineligible for baseball his sophomore year.

That's when Hank Watkins, his former line coach at Abilene, called. Watkins by then was the line coach at the University of Houston and offered Green a scholarship to play football for the Cougars. Green was married, and Watkins also secured a job for his wife.

So Green transferred to Houston to play football. "I redshirted my first year. The next year, I was starting. The third or fourth game of the year we went to Miami to play in that old wooden Orange Bowl. One of my own players hit me in the head and knocked me out." Green had a severe concussion, and his football career was over.

"They flew me back to Houston," he said, "but it was several days before I got my memory back. At that same time, my wife found out she was pregnant. She asked me what I thought about having a baby. I was so excited, and then ten minutes later she'd ask me the same thing. I was the happiest guy ever having a baby because every time she told me it was like the first time I'd heard it."

Although his football and baseball careers were over, Green remained at the University of Houston and finished his degree in business in 1961. He became an insurance adjuster, working in Houston, Dallas, Seguin, and Haskell before moving back to Abilene. He spent the last eighteen years of his career as an adjuster for Farm Bureau Insurance in Abilene before retiring.

Green worked the last twelve years in the same office with his good friend and former teammate Cullen Hunt, who was a starting tackle on the 1954 team. "Now we play golf together every day," Green said.

GLYNN GREGORY
All-state back 1955 and 1956

Glynn Gregory is considered one of the greatest athletes in Abilene history. He was the only player to be named a two-time all-state selection during the Moser era, was also honored as the state's top high school football player, and was named a high school all-American in 1956. He was a three-sport standout, playing football, basketball, and baseball for the Eagles, earning all-district honors in all three sports and all-state in football and baseball.

After high school, Gregory played football and baseball at Southern Methodist University and then spent three seasons (1961-63) with the Dallas Cowboys. He was a teammate of Don Meredith at SMU and with the Cowboys.

But Gregory's career—and life—nearly ended on Thanksgiving Day in 1955. The Eagles were scheduled to play their traditional Thanksgiving Day game against San Angelo at Fair Park Stadium.

"My mother had contracted tuberculosis," Gregory said, "so she was in a hospital in San Angelo. My dad would get up early to open his service station, and then he'd call me to make sure I was up."

Gregory said the telephone was on a desk in a hallway that ran between the bathroom, his parents' bedroom, and his bedroom.

"I was going to a restaurant to eat a good breakfast before the

Glynn Gregory

game," he said. "My dad called to wake me up. I picked up the phone in the hallway, and the next thing I know I'm on my back in the bathroom. I staggered back to bed, and then the phone rang again. It was my dad. He asked what happened, and I told him I fainted. The next thing I remember I'm waking up on the floor again and crawling back to bed."

Gregory said his next memory was his father shaking him, trying to wake him up. Gregory's father had driven from his service station on the north side of Abilene to their home on South First Street.

"He told me later that he broke every speeding record trying to get there," Gregory said. "I guess he smelled it (a gas leak) because he took me outside and opened up all the doors and windows. Then he called Dr. (Dub) Sibley (the Abilene team doctor), and he said to bring me to his house."

It was later determined that there was a crack in the pipe that took the exhaust from a floor furnace out of the house. That had caused the carbon monoxide leak in the Gregory home.

"Dr. Sibley examined me," Gregory said. "He told my dad if he had waited ten or twenty more minutes, that would have been it. I was extremely fortunate."

Despite his scare that morning, Gregory played that afternoon against San Angelo. In fact, it was one of the best games in his remarkable career. He intercepted three passes, rushed for sixty-six yards on just four carries, scored two touchdowns including a forty-six-yard TD run, and kicked all five extra points in a 35-6 victory over the Bobcats.

Unlike most of the players on the Eagles' team, Gregory didn't grow up in Abilene. He moved to Abilene from Paris, east of Dallas, prior to entering the eighth grade.

"My dad's younger brother was in Pearl Harbor," Gregory said. "When he got out of the Navy, he went to college and then moved to Abilene to work in the oil business. He kept encouraging my dad to move to Abilene, and finally we did. We moved to Abilene the day I graduated from Paris East Junior High. I went to the eighth and ninth grade at South Junior High. My dad was working in the oil field as a roughneck when he got hurt and lost the sight in one eye. After he recovered from that, he bought a service station when I was in the ninth grade."

After his playing career ended with the Dallas Cowboys, Gregory spent thirty-one years with The Equitable Life Insurance Company in Dallas before retiring. He now works in development for the Texas Scottish Rite Hospital for Children.

"I'm a fund-raiser," he said. "I call on donors and people who have remembered the hospital in estate planning. I cover the state of Texas. I love it. I've been involved with the hospital since 1969. It's a special place."

STUART PEAKE
All-state guard 1956

Stuart Peake claims he's lived a charmed life, and it might be hard to disagree with him.

He is the only player who started every game on both offense and defense for Abilene's three state championship teams. He lost only one game during a three-year high school career and earned all-state and all-American honors as a senior.

After high school, Peake went to the University of Texas as a member of Darrell Royal's first recruiting class. He went to medical school after his playing career with the Longhorns and is now a successful intraventional radiologist in Dallas.

Peake gives a great deal of credit for the Eagles' phenomenal success to assistant coach Hank Watkins. "Hank was the mastermind of our rule blocking and defense. He was phenomenal. He was every bit as responsible as Coach Moser for our success."

Peake hasn't forgotten his old line coach, either. For the last fifteen years, he has driven to San Marcos to pick up Watkins before

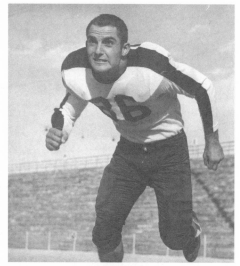

Stuart Peake

every home football game at the University of Texas. The two sit together. "We've been doing it so long, I can't remember when I started."

Although Peake played guard, he was one of the fastest runners on the team. He was clocked in 9.8 in the 100-yard dash and ran on the Eagles' sprint relay team in track. So why wasn't he a running back?

"In spring training my junior year, they tried to make me a fullback," Peake said, laughing. "I'd trip on a blade of glass. I was terrible. Finally, Coach Watkins came to me and said, 'Do you want to be a second-rate fullback or an all-state guard?' I said I wanted to be an all-state guard. I knew what I was doing there."

Peake said his best game was Abilene's 33-13 win over favored Tyler in the 1955 state championship game. "I had a ton of tackles. But the radio announcer (legendary Southwest Conference announcer Kern Tips) had the numbers mixed up, and he gave credit for every one of my tackles to Vance McFadden. And he wasn't even suited up."

The Tyler game may have been Peake's best performance, but his most memorable moment occurred the year after he graduated.

Peake, who had his pilot's license, was a freshman at the University of Texas and rented a small Cessna to fly from Austin to Amarillo to see his younger brother Alan and the Eagles take on the Amarillo Sandies in the 1957 quarterfinals. The Sandies were appropriately nicknamed that day; the game finished in a sandstorm.

"A blue norther' blew in," Peake recalled. "I was flying directly into it. The wind was so strong I probably wasn't going fifteen mph. When I looked down, the cars on the road were making better time than I was, and I was about to run out of gas. I was somewhere between Childress and Amarillo when I saw a Humble gas station down there. So I landed the airplane on the highway and taxied up next the station.

"Golden Esso was the hottest gas back then. Well, the guy at the station came out, and I said I wonder if I could get some Golden Esso. He said, 'Most guys just drive up to the pump.' I got gas and flew on to the game. But I had to wait until the storm blew past the next day before I could take off again."

Peake said he remembers that John Young played a "phenomenal game" as the outmanned Eagles upset No. 1-ranked Amarillo for their forty-ninth consecutive victory.

JIMMY CARPENTER
All-state back 1956

Jimmy Carpenter is remembered for a number of outstanding achievements during his career at Abilene High School. He was an all-state back in 1956 and a three-year letterman in football and baseball on teams that won five state championships and narrowly missed another one. He is a member of the Big Country Athletic Hall of Fame and the Texas High School Football Hall of Fame.

Carpenter wore No. 71, a number usually worn by linemen rather than a star halfback. There is a story behind that No. 71.

Jimmy Carpenter

"I was bashful," Carpenter said. "During two-a-days my sophomore year, we had to form a line to get equipment, and I got at the back of the line. By the time they got to me, they had run out of the good helmets, so they gave me an old leather helmet. I wore it two or three days before Coach Moser came to me asked how come I was wearing that old helmet. I said that was the one they gave me."

"I'll see if we can get you a better helmet," Moser told Carpenter, who was then issued a newer helmet like the rest of the team wore.

The same thing happened when the Eagles handed out jerseys. Although he was one of the fastest players on the team and made the varsity as a sophomore at running back and defensive back, the jerseys usually worn by the backs had already been issued by the time Carpenter reached the front of the line. So they gave him No. 71.

"I was just glad to get a real jersey," he said. "I wore it the whole time in high school."

It may be safe to assume that Carpenter is the fastest player ever to wear No. 71. Under today's rules, a running back has to wear a number smaller than 50.

Carpenter went on to play at the University of Oklahoma. He was selected to play in several college all-star games and was drafted by the Houston Oilers. But he elected not to continue his football career, instead taking a job in the oil business with Amoco Production in the Rocky Mountains, living in Denver and Billings, Montana. Nearly twenty years ago, he quit his job and returned to Oklahoma, going to work for himself in the oil business. He has lived in Edmond, Oklahoma, ever since.

Carpenter's father was a local contractor in Abilene and always employed seven or eight Abilene football players in the summer, including his son. "It was hard work," Carpenter recalled. "We'd dig ditches and haul concrete. We were in the middle of a drought and it was over 100 degrees every day in the summer." That was how Carpenter and his teammates got in shape for the upcoming season.

Carpenter calls his years at Abilene High among the highlights of his life. "It was a great time. As I look back on it, Abilene High was pretty good in everything."

RUFUS KING
All-state tackle 1956

Rufus King was named a first-team all-state tackle as a senior in 1956. Not bad for a guy who didn't play tackle. King, a two-year starter on both offense and defense for the Eagles, did play defensive tackle and was a starting offensive tackle as a junior. As a senior, however, he moved to tight end.

"They moved Kenny Schmidt to the other end," King said, "so we were really playing with a center, two guards and four tackles. We didn't throw much, and if we did it was to (halfbacks) Gregory and Carpenter."

King said the Abilene quarterbacks threw only two passes to him all year. One, early in the season, went over his head. The other pass attempt fell incomplete in the state championship game, but Corpus Christi Ray was flagged for pass interference on the play.

Rufus King spent most of his football career playing next to his brother Boyd. Boyd was the starting right tackle for the Eagles, while Rufus was lined up next to him at right end. The two went on to Rice to play college football, where both were three-year starters—Boyd at center and Rufus at guard. They also roomed together at Rice.

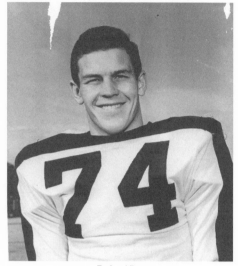

Rufus King

"A lot of people thought we were twins," said Rufus, laughing, "but we weren't. Boyd was the ugly one. We were as different as day and night, but we were always together."

Boyd was actually a year younger than Rufus, but they were in the same class.

Boyd died of colon cancer in 2000.

When Rufus graduated from Rice, he turned down an opportunity to play in the Canadian Football League and instead went to work for the Aetna insurance company. He spent eight years at Aetna before opening his own company in Houston in 1968. In 1993, King, an insurance broker, sold his agency and moved back to Abilene, where he owns his own business.

"Abilene has always been my home," he said. "Even when I lived in Houston, Abilene was home."

King said he feels fortunate to have played his entire football career for Moser and legendary Rice coach Jess Neely.

"We beat Texas twice during my three years on the varsity," King said. The Owls went to the Sugar Bowl during King's senior year.

"We were 7-3," he said. "We beat Florida, Texas and Texas A&M, and we lost by just three points to Georgia Tech, Baylor and

Arkansas." Ole Miss defeated Rice, 14-6, in the Sugar Bowl.

King gives a lot of credit for his success to Hank Watkins, the Eagles' line coach.

"When we played Corpus Christi Ray in the state championship game, Sonny Wharton, the defensive end across from me, weighed about 220. He went on to play at Baylor. I only weighed about 190, and I couldn't handle him. Coach Watkins told me to start false blocking. That's when you put your head on one side to block him, and then you whip your tail around. Finally, we started having success.

"Hank was the finest line coach I've ever seen. He taught me so many tricks. I was so far ahead of the other freshmen when I got to Rice. He hasn't gotten as much credit for our success as he deserves."

JIMMY PERRY
All-state end 1957

Jimmy Perry caught only one touchdown pass during his senior year, but it couldn't have come at a more critical time. He made a tremendous leaping catch in the middle of the field near the thirty-eight-yard line, then wheeled away from one tackler and dashed to the end zone, completing a sixty-one-yard touchdown play in the second quarter of Abilene's quarterfinal game with top-ranked Amarillo in 1957.

The Freddy Martinez-to-Perry pass play tied the score at 14-14. The Eagles then pulled away in the second half for the improbable 33-14 victory, which turned out to be the final win in Abilene's record forty-nine-game winning streak.

"That kept us in the game long enough for us to get organized (at halftime)," Moser said after the game.

Perry caught just seven passes for 190 yards and the one score as a senior, but his efforts as both a blocker and receiver were enough to gain the lanky 6-5, 180-pounder first team all-state honors that season. That may have been a bit of surprise to some since Perry spent his junior season playing behind starting ends Kenny Schmidt and Rufus King.

"He really came on," assistant coach Wally Bullington said of Perry. "He was a pleasant surprise, how he developed from the year before."

Perry's receiving numbers probably wouldn't be considered all-state caliber today, but the 1950s were an era when teams didn't throw the ball much. And the Eagles passed more to their half-backs out of the split-T formation than they did their ends.

"Jim was a good tight end," Bullington said. "He was a tall kid, a good basketball player. He had good hands and was a good receiver. He was also a good blocker for his size. He was a good competitor."

Jimmy Perry

MICHAEL BRYANT
All-state tackle 1957

Michael Bryant was one of the biggest players during the Moser era in Abilene. Bryant was 6-4 and weighed 220, although the official roster listed him as 198 pounds. "Moser wouldn't show anyone over 200 pounds," he said.

Bryant, who now lives in Fort Worth, was named all-state at tackle as a senior in 1957. He signed with SMU after high school, but a series of head injuries during his freshman year ended his football career. "I kept breaking helmets," said Bryant, who believes his concussions actually date back to his high school playing days. "I couldn't even walk."

Bryant, who has spent his career since football in banking and the trucking business, credits the Eagles' success to an outstanding group of assistant coaches. "I was from the wrong side of town, so it was harder to make it. But Wally Bullington didn't care. He was a helluva coach. Shorty Lawson, Nat Gleaton, and Harold Brinson were good coaches, too."

Bryant also believes the consistency of Moser's program was part of the reason for the Eagles' success. "We ran the same plays from the fourth grade up. There was no question who you blocked. We were doing zone blocking. No one else used it."

He said the Eagles didn't have much of a weight program back then, but players were required to have summer jobs. Bryant worked for a construction company. Coach Moser "wanted you working hard, doing physical labor and working outside, so the heat wouldn't bother you."

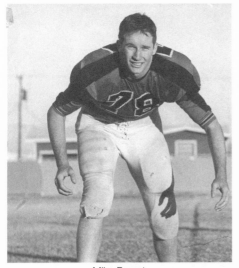
Mike Bryant

He said the Eagles also did a lot of agility drills and climbed ropes, which helped the linemen's quickness. "Many times I'd blocked for Chuck Colvin. He'd run past me and I'd catch him by the time he got to the end zone."

Bryant said he met his wife, the former Crystal Ragsdale, when she was a South Junior High cheerleader and he was a sophomore at Abilene High. They have been married forty-two years.

"I had a good time," he said, looking back on his high school career. "They were marvelous years. I didn't have any money, but everything seemed to turn out right. We never thought about losing."

BILL SIDES
All-state fullback 1957

Bill Sides didn't really know how to act when Highland Park tied Abilene, 20-20, in the 1957 semifinals, snapping the Eagles' forty-nine-game winning streak and bid for a fourth consecutive state championship.

"I'd never lost a game before—from seventh grade through my senior year," said Sides, who now lives in suburban Atlanta and is still involved in the insurance business. "I'd always been a starter, too, except for my sophomore year."

Sides was the back-up fullback on the Eagles' 1955 state championship team as a sophomore. "I played behind James Welch that year. He was a good mentor. He went on to play for SMU and the Baltimore Colts. He was a good, solid blocking fullback. I learned a lot from him."

Sides was mostly a blocking fullback for all-state halfbacks Jimmy Carpenter and Glynn Gregory as a junior in 1956 when the Eagles captured their third straight state title. As a senior in 1957, Sides became Abilene's marquee back, rushing for 1,057 yards.

Bill Sides

"We weren't supposed to have a team like the past," he said of the 1957 Eagles, "but we still had enough guys who had been together during a four-year period. And we had that tradition."

Sides was offered a scholarship to play football at Texas Christian University but turned it down. "Bob Lilly took me around the campus on my visit to TCU. Abe Martin (TCU's coach) wanted me to be a pulling guard. He didn't want me as a fullback. He said he wanted to beef me up and make me a pulling guard. I thought if everyone I would have to block was the size of Bob Lilly, I didn't want any part of that."

Instead, Sides, who said he was "5-10, 170, dripping wet," walked on at the University of Texas. A leg injury cut short his football career at Texas although he played baseball for the Longhorns.

Sides still remembers his first experience as an Abilene Eagle. "It was spring training, my ninth grade year. We went up to work with the high school team. They scared us to death. I couldn't believe I was working against guys like Sam Caudle and Stuart Peake. They were my idols. We had all these head-on blocking and tackling drills. I thought I'd be all right if I can go through two weeks and not get killed."

He did more than survive. He was a two-year starter, a three-year letterman and a first team all-state selection as a senior.

He said the Eagles were like a well-oiled offensive machine. "The whole line would fire off together. They beat people off the ball. We'd run the three-dive or the four-dive play and make four, five or six yards every time. We'd make first downs in two plays. It was fun to watch."

Sides attributes much of his success in life after football to Moser. "I had a good father, but Coach Moser influenced my life more than anyone other than my father with what he instilled in me. I've been successful, and I attribute that to being competitive. A lot of that comes from my high school coach."

DAVID PARKS
All-state end 1959

David Parks became a star wide receiver in the National Football League. But that wasn't his goal when he was growing up.

"Sam Caudle lived a half-block away from me," said Parks, who was in junior high when Abilene was in the midst of winning three consecutive state championships. "He was my hero. He and so many guys like Carpenter, Gregory, the King brothers, and Stuart Peake. Watching them, all I wanted to be was good enough to be an Abilene High Eagle. I knew if I was good enough to be an Abilene High Eagle, I'd be a decent player."

Parks went on to be much more. He was Moser's final all-state selection at Abilene, earning honors as a senior in 1959. Parks signed with Texas Tech, where he is a member of that school's Hall of Fame as one of the leading receivers in Red Raider history. The San Francisco 49ers then made him the first pick in the 1965 NFL draft.

In 2003, Parks joined two of his boyhood idols—Gregory and Carpenter, along with two of his former coaches, Moser and Blackburn—in the Big Country Athletic Hall of Fame.

"That means a lot to me," said Parks, who now lives in Dallas. "I've never been awed by the pros or college players, and I've been around the best. But when I get around that bunch, I'm in awe. I knew they had high standards. Those guys were role models. They were fantastic people, and they did what it took. What they accomplished is unbelievable. Football to me was not an individual thing; it was a team thing. I realized so much out of it. Being named all-state was nice, but I'm embarrassed when I receive individual recognition. I never compare myself to those guys, like Sam Caudle and Stuart Peake. They were so much better. That's what made Moser's system do so well because those guys believed in the team concept."

David Parks

Parks said some athletes are born with greatness. But he said he had to work hard for everything he accomplished. He attributes much of his success to Moser and his staff, especially Bullington.

"They had a huge impact on my life," he said. "I didn't know how much until I got away from it. When I was in the NFL, I was still using the same basic technique that I learned from Coach Moser and his staff."

Parks said Wally Bullington worked with him in the off-season to improve his skills. "He played a big part in what happened to me."

Parks, who moved to Abilene from St. Joe, Texas, in the fifth grade, said he would have never had that kind of success had his father not taken a job as a tool pusher with an oil company in Abilene.

Success didn't come immediately for Parks. He quit the football team in the eighth grade and wasn't a starter in the ninth grade. His junior high coach told him that there wasn't any need for him to go out for football that spring because they would only use him as a "tackling dummy" at Abilene High.

"I was a sub on the last team that spring," Parks said.

He wasn't even on the junior varsity roster when it came time for physicals that fall. But by the third game of the 1957 season, he had earned a spot in the starting lineup on the junior varsity team.

Moser planned to move Parks up to the varsity for the showdown against number one-ranked Amarillo in the playoffs later that season, but Parks said he had a "D" in Latin. "Coach Moser called me in and said I couldn't make the trip because of that 'D'. Then he asked me what I was doing taking Latin."

"I don't know," Parks replied. "I needed a foreign language, and (Charles) McCook was taking it."

"McCook is going to be a doctor (he is currently a dentist in Post)," Moser said. "If you need a foreign language, why don't you take Spanish?"

Parks dropped Latin, and the rest is history. He became a two-year, two-way starter at Abilene High. After a great career at Texas Tech, he spent four seasons with the 49ers, finishing runner-up for Rookie of the Year in the NFL and once leading the league in receiving.

He played out his option after his fourth season at San Francisco and signed with the New Orleans Saints. "That was a bad career move," Parks said. "I left one of the best lines in football and left a great, great quarterback (John Brodie) to go to a second-year expansion club without a lot of talent."

After five seasons with the Saints, Parks played one year with the Houston Oilers before finishing out his eleven-year pro football career with the Southern California Sun in the World Football League.

CHAPTER 11

From Backup to the NFL

Receiving accolades in high school doesn't necessarily mean success in college. Likewise, a lack of post-season honors doesn't mean a player doesn't have a chance to move on to play college and even professional football.

James Welch is a perfect example. Welch, the fullback on Abilene's 1955 state championship team, never even earned all-district recognition, let alone all-state honors. But he went on to enjoy a nine-year career in the National Football League, the most successful professional career of any of the players on the Eagles' three state championship teams.

"I didn't have a chance to make all-district," Welch said, "because Midland had Wahoo McDaniel, who was an all-state fullback. He was a big load."

Welch didn't even move up to the varsity until the end of his junior year. "I played linebacker on the JV. At the end of the year, one of the linebackers was injured, so they moved me up to the varsity for the last game of the season and then the playoffs."

He was moved to fullback as a senior but didn't get his first start until the Odessa game, midway through the season. Henry Colwell was starting at fullback, and junior speedsters Jimmy Carpenter and Glynn Gregory were the halfbacks. Carpenter sprained his ankle before the Odessa game, so Moser moved Colwell to halfback and inserted Welch into the starting lineup at fullback.

What followed was one of the greatest games in Abilene history. "On the first play of the game, we called a draw play," Welch recalled "It opened up like no one was there. The rest of the night, we kept pounding them. That was the beginning of my career."

James Welch

Welch finished with 233 yards rushing that night, a total that remains the fourth best single-game rushing performance in Abilene High football history.

He went on to Southern Methodist University, where he played fullback and linebacker for the Mustangs., then was drafted by Baltimore and spent nine years in the NFL, eight with the Colts and one season with the Detroit Lions.

He played running back as a rookie, then moved to defensive back and started six years in the secondary for the Colts, where he was a teammate of legendary quarterback Johnny Unitas and a member of Don Shula's first team as a head coach. The Colts never won a championship during Welch's tenure with the team, having the misfortune of playing in the same division as the powerful Green Bay Packers.

"In 1965, we tied with Green Bay so we had a playoff to see who would play in the championship," Welch said. "Unitas was hurt, so we moved Tom Matte, a halfback who had played quarterback at Ohio State, to quarterback. I still think we beat them. They kicked a field goal to tie it up. It was a yard wide, but they called it good, and then they beat us in overtime. I have both a bad and a good memory of that."

Welch has nothing but wonderful memories of Abilene, however. "The best memories of my life are my senior year. Moser was a great teacher, a great tactician. He outsmarted the other coaches. Some teams had better players, but we were well-coached. We always had a great game plan. He was a great motivator, and everyone loved him. He could give you that look, and you'd want to crawl under the table. But I was fortunate to play for him.

"Our coach in college (Bill Meek) was several generations behind Moser. Don Meredith was our quarterback at SMU, but Meek didn't know what to do with him. We'd always blow the big ones."

Welch landed a job as a retail stockbroker in the off-season during his second year with the Colts. "I stayed with that when I retired from football. Then I moved to New York and became an institutional trader. That's what I did for nearly thirty years until it was time to hang it up." He and his wife moved to Trophy Club, near Fort Worth, to be close to their children and grandchildren.

Welch, who claimed his dreams came true by winning a state championship and getting to play football at SMU and in the NFL, said he doesn't have memories of specific plays or games from his career at Abilene High.

"More of my memories are about teammates and Chuck Moser," Welch said. "He was it."

CHAPTER 12

1958-59: The Forgotten Years

The final two seasons of Moser's remarkable seven-year run at Abilene High have often been overlooked in the aftermath of the Eagles' three consecutive state championships and a state-record forty-nine-game winning streak. But they shouldn't be.

There were plenty of other accomplishments in 1958 and 1959. Those two teams produced the most acclaimed professional football player in Abilene history and one of its top baseball players who made the major leagues. Abilene won two more district championships, giving the Eagles six consecutive district titles from 1954-59, a feat that has been equaled only once in the long, storied history of the "Little Southwest Conference." Odessa Permian won six in a row from 1980-85.

As the 1958 season began, the Eagles were coming off the heartbreaking 20-20 tie to Highland Park in the semifinals a year earlier. Although it was a tie, the Scots advanced to the state championship contest because they had five penetrations of the twenty-yard line to just three for the Eagles.

Abilene's streak of unbeaten games, however, stood at fifty as the Eagles prepared to face San Antonio Jefferson in the 1958 season opener at Fair Park. Abilene returned only one starter—halfback Stan Cozby—on offense and just two starters—defensive tackle Frank Aycock and cornerback Charles Harrison, who also started at fullback-—on defense.

The season opener was a thriller. Abilene rallied from a 26-16 deficit to take a 28-26 victory. Cozby's fifty-four-yard touchdown run in the third quarter pulled the Eagles to within four, and Harrison's one-yard run with 9:20 remaining produced the game-winner.

The Eagles also took advantage of a new rule that came into effect for the first time in the 1958 season. A team was awarded two points if it ran or passed for the conversion after a touchdown rather than the one point it received for an extra-point kick. Prior to 1958, a team received just one point, regardless of whether it kicked, ran, or passed the ball. Abilene scored two-point conversions after each of its first two touchdowns of the game.

Jefferson's twenty-six points were the most scored against an Abilene team since the 35-13 loss to Breckenridge in 1954, the last loss suffered by the Warbirds. The Eagles had played fifty-one consecutive games since that third game of the 1954 season without losing on the field.

EAGLES ARE SHUT OUT

The Eagles' fifty-one-game unbeaten streak was smashed the next week when neighboring Sweetwater blanked Abilene 19-0 at Sweetwater's Mustang Bowl. New *Abilene Reporter-News* sports editor Fred Sanner noted the historic loss in the next morning's paper: "It was the first time that Coach Chuck Moser's team had failed to score since he came to Abilene at the first of the 1953 season. It was only his fourth defeat in his Abilene career."

It was Sweetwater's first win over Abilene since 1948. Moser wasn't all that surprised, however.

"I saw the handwriting on the wall when they gave us such a tough time last year," Moser said the next day. "You know, I looked around the dining room when we fed our kids last night and Frank Aycock was the only boy who was with us when we played over there in 1956. And Sweetwater had eight boys who have played against us three years now."

Two nights later, Moser received a standing ovation at the Eagle Booster Club meeting at the Coca-Cola Auditorium.

"I don't know whether you realize it or not," Moser told the booster club, "but 500 high school teams played last week and 250 of them got beat. It doesn't hurt to get beat once. It's when you get beat twice that it hurts. It gets to be like a habit and we don't want it to be a habit."

That was never a problem with Moser. The Eagles didn't lose again until the state quarterfinals. The two losses to Odessa and Pampa back in 1953, Moser's first season in Abilene, marked the only time the Eagles lost back-to-back games in the Moser Era.

Abilene resumed its winning ways the next week, blanking Lubbock Monterey, 34-0, and then shutting out Breckenridge 22-0. Abilene's defense—led by Frank Aycock, Don Hughes, Leroy Johnson, Ray Crumpler, Jerry Osborn, and Jimmy Gilstrap—held Breckenridge to only thirty-two yards rushing and thirty-two passing.

The 1958 Eagles were starting to look like the earlier Abilene teams as they closed out non-district play with a 52-8 thrashing of Austin Travis and a 36-0 shutout of Waco.

DISTRICT SWEEP

The Eagles, who hadn't lost a district game since the 7-6 setback to Pampa in 1953, opened District 2-AAAA play with a 38-8 win over Big Spring. After a week off, Abilene mauled Odessa 34-14 and followed that with a 29-6 win over Midland. Abilene then completed the regular season with a tough 12-0 win over San Angelo. The Saturday afternoon victory was a defensive struggle, but the Eagles scored a touchdown with eighteen seconds left before halftime and added a final score with six seconds remaining in the fourth quarter to clinch their fifth consecutive district championship.

Don Hughes, playing in the line, spearheaded the Abilene defense with eight critical tackles, including two for losses. He also had an interception as the Eagles posted their fifth shutout in their last eight games after being held scoreless themselves in week two of the season by Sweetwater.

Abilene had to travel to El Paso for a bi-district match-up with Ysleta, but they kept soaring, defeating the Indians 40-6. Next up was powerful Wichita Falls in the Class AAAA quarterfinals.

The Coyotes whipped Abilene 34-6, ending the Eagles' nine-game winning streak. Wichita Falls' numbers in the victory looked more like an Abilene-type performance than those of the Eagles. The Coyotes' single-wing offense rolled up 235 yards rushing, while their defense held Abilene to an uncharacteristic fifty-three yards on the ground.

Wichita Falls went on to win the state championship, beating defending champion Highland Park in the semifinals and then blasting Pasadena 48-6 in the title game.

Despite the loss, it had been quite a year for the Eagles, whose defense allowed an average of just seven points per game.

Before the season began, Moser had accurately predicted how the 1958 campaign would come out. He had told those close to him that Abilene would probably lose to Sweetwater or Breckenridge early in the year, have a good chance to win district, but Wichita Falls would probably "knock us out of the playoffs." That's exactly what happened.

David Parks at end, Frank Aycock at tackle, Don Hughes at guard, Arch Ratliff at center, Freddie Martinez at quarterback, and Charles Harrison at running back were first team all-district selections. Stan Cozby was named the Eagle Player of the Year at the annual football banquet. The Abilene coaching staff was awarded $6,500 in cash and gift certificates for the team's fifth consecutive district championship.

For the first time in Moser's six years at Abilene, however, the Eagles failed to land a player in the Class AAAA all-state first team. Five Eagles—Parks, Aycock, Hughes, Cozby, and Harrison—were named honorable mention all-state.

Harrison went on to make quite a name for himself in another sport. He played both football and baseball at Texas Tech, then enjoyed a five-year baseball career in the major leagues. The right-handed hitting first baseman was known as Chuck Harrison during his five seasons with the Houston Astros (1965-67) and Kansas City Royals (1969, 1971). He had a .238 batting average, hitting 17 home runs and driving in 85 runs in 328 games during his big-league career.

CHANGING TIMES

As the Eagles began preparation for the 1959 season, fans knew it was the beginning of a new era. But they had no idea it would mark the end of another.

The team moved to a new home, known as Public Schools Stadium, in 1959. The new 15,000-seat stadium, located on South Eleventh Street across from the West Texas Fairgrounds on the east side of Abilene, was designed after Rice Stadium in Houston, home of the Rice Owls and site of one of the early Super Bowls.

Fred Sanner, sports editor for the *Abilene Reporter-News* at the time, wrote a column suggesting the stadium's name be changed to Shotwell Stadium, in honor of former Abilene coach Pete Shotwell. Shortly after the first season, the stadium was officially renamed Shotwell Stadium. It marked the first time the Abilene Independent School District had named a building or facility for a person still living.

Forty-five years later, Shotwell Stadium is still the home field for the AISD's two high schools. The stadium recently received major renovations, including the installation of SafePlay turf in 2002 and a new state-of-the-art scoreboard in 2003. New locker rooms, press box and paved parking lots are also planned for the stadium, built initially thanks to the growing popularity of Moser's successful Eagles.

Abilene successfully opened the new stadium on Sept. 11 by edging San Antonio Jefferson in a thriller, 14-12. The story in the next morning's *Abilene Reporter-News* didn't mention his name, but San Antonio Jefferson's lineup that night included a sophomore who became a Pro Football Hall of Fame selection himself. Tommy Nobis, an all-American at the University of Texas and an all-pro linebacker for the Atlanta Falcons, played his first high school game at Shotwell Stadium.

Abilene quarterback Charles McCook put his name in the record book when he scored the first touchdown in the new stadium. McCook's three-yard run with 2:24 left in the second quarter and Bobby Austin's extra-point kick gave the Eagles a 7-0 lead.

Seconds later, Abilene recovered a fumble, and the Eagles used a trick play to strike for another score. McCook threw a ten-yard pass to Parks, who lateraled back to Sarge Newman on a hook-and-lateral play. Newman ran for a touchdown, completing the forty-four-yard play with 1:51 remaining.

Abilene's 14-0 halftime lead held up despite two second-half Jefferson touchdowns as David Parks recovered a fumble on the two-point conversion attempt to tie the game.

On the Thursday night following the Eagles' opener, Hardin-Simmons University faced North Texas State at the new stadium. Like the Abilene-San Antonio Jefferson game, HSU's game against North Texas also featured a future pro star. Running back Abner Haynes led North Texas to a 46-24 romp over the Cowboys before a crowd of 11,500. Haynes went on star for the Dallas Texans and Kansas City Chiefs in the American Football League.

The next night, Abilene played its second game in the new stadium, beating Sweetwater 29-12 before 14,000 fans, the largest crowd to watch an Eagles' home game. McCook passed for two touchdowns and ran for another to lead Abilene to its second victory of the season.

A COUPLE OF SQUEAKERS

After a week off, Abilene traveled to Breckenridge to face the Buckaroos. The Eagles had beaten rival Breckenridge four years in a row since the 1954 loss, the game that preceded the record win streak. This year's match-up produced the closest game in recent years, however.

Abilene scored on its first two possessions and took a 14-7 half-time lead. Fullback Mike Wayman's dive for a two-point conversion after the second touchdown proved to be the difference in the game, although no one realized it at the time.

Breckenridge, ranked number one in the state in Class AAA, dominated the second half, but the Buckaroos didn't score until talented quarterback Jerry Gibson hit Billy West with a five-yard touchdown pass with 2:40 left in the game, trimming the Eagles' lead to 14-13. Buckaroos coach Emory Bellard then rolled the dice, going for a two-point conversion to try to win the game rather than kicking the extra point for a potential tie. Abilene defensive backs David Winkles and T.A. Buchanan jarred end Jack Stephens loose from a two-point conversion pass from Gibson and the Eagles had a one-point victory, improving their record to 3-0.

San Antonio Alamo Heights (4-0) was Abilene's next opponent in a battle of unbeaten teams. It was no match. The Eagles beat the Mules 42-0 and climbed past defending champion Wichita Falls to the number one spot in the Class AAAA poll.

Bobby Austin accounted for all thirteen of Abilene's points in their next outing, a 13-12 win over Waco at Public Schools Stadium. Austin caught a thirty-six-yard TD pass from McCook and scored the tying touchdown on a ten-yard run up the middle in the third quarter to tie the score. He then booted the winning PAT, giving the Eagles their third win by one or two points in the team's five non-district games.

DISTRICT STREAK ENDS

Abilene opened District 2-AAAA play with three straight shutouts—36-0 over Big Spring, 44-0 over the district's newest team, Odessa Permian, and 7-0 over Odessa High.

The Eagles were unbeaten, 8-0 overall and 3-0 in district, and ranked number one in the state. It was like old times in Abilene.

The *Abilene Reporter-News* said the Eagles "iced" their sixth consecutive district championship and sixth straight playoff berth with a 28-7 win over Midland High. It was a good choice of verbs because

9,000 fans shivered in Public Schools Stadium in 29-degree temperatures that felt even colder thanks to a 25-mph north wind.

In the final game of the regular season, the improbable happened. San Angelo upset Abilene 13-0 in a game played in San Angelo. It was the Bobcats' first win over Abilene in ten years and the Eagles' first district loss since that 7-6 setback to Pampa in the middle of the 1953 season. Abilene had two offensive starters and five defensive starters on the sideline with injuries, but no one was making excuses.

The loss meant Abilene had to share the district title with Odessa, but the Eagles earned the playoff berth thanks to their 7-0 win over the Bronchos two weeks earlier.

END OF THE ROAD

A bi-district playoff berth meant another encounter with El Paso's best team, and that usually meant a lopsided victory. The Eagles routed El Paso Ysleta 45-0.

David Winkles returned the game's opening kickoff ninety-nine yards for a touchdown. Then, on Ysleta's first possession, David Parks intercepted a pass and returned it sixty yards for a touchdown. Abilene had a 12-0 lead before it had even run a play offensively. Abilene's defense held Ysleta to a minus-three yards rushing in the second half.

The Eagles faced defending state champion Wichita Falls for the second year in a row in the quarterfinals. When the Coyotes ousted Abilene 26-12, long-time Wichita Falls coach Joe Golding called the victory "my greatest thrill" because his Coyotes had just become the first team to beat the Eagles twice since Moser came to Abilene seven years earlier.

Abilene led 12-6 at halftime, but Wichita Falls took advantage of the Eagles' miscues in the second half. The Coyotes recovered two Abilene fumbles and intercepted three passes.

The 1959 season had ended with Abilene's second straight 10-2 season and an Eagles' loss in the quarterfinals for the second straight year.

A month later—on January 15, 1960—the greatest era in Texas high school football history came to an end when Moser announced his resignation. He was named athletic director for the Abilene Independent School District. Bullington was selected as Moser's replacement at the same time, while it was also announced that Moser would have a hand in naming the coach for the new South Side high school, later named Cooper High School, that would open the next fall.

Not only was it the end of the Moser Era; the conclusion of the 1959 football season also marked the end of the one-high-school era in Abilene. Abilene would never be the same.

CHAPTER 13

Moser's Legacy

Doris Moser, Chuck's widow, now lives in a nursing home in Boerne, near her youngest daughter Glenn. Although her memory has faded some, Mrs. Moser is quick to respond when asked what she remembered most about her years in Abilene.

"Winning," Mrs. Moser answered. "When you lose, you go in the back yard and pout. Chuck would take the children out for donuts on Saturday morning if they won. No win, no donuts. Donuts were important."

In his book *Autumn's Mightiest Legions*, Harold Ratliff, the long-time Texas sports editor for the Associated Press bureau in Dallas, said Moser had a "habit of going downtown to shake everybody's hand when he won but to work in the back yard at his home when he lost."

"That first year in McAllen we didn't win very many football games, but we had the prettiest back yard in town, roses, flowers, shrubs all over the place," Doris Moser told Ratliff. "At Abilene we had a very poor yard because we seldom ever lost. But it was worth it."

Moser, who died in 1995, compiled an incredible 141-29-4 coaching record in his sixteen-year career, including a 78-7-2 mark in seven seasons in Abilene. His stint in Abilene included six straight district titles (1594-59) and three consecutive Class AAAA state championships (1954-56). Each mark has been equaled only once—and never surpassed—in the past fifty years.

The Eagles' forty-nine straight victories from 1954-57 set a national interscholastic record at the time. It remained the state's longest winning streak until Class 2A Celina, led by coach G.A. Moore, topped Abilene's winning streak in 2001. Celina, which moved up to Class 3A in 2002, finally had its win streak stopped at sixty-eight with a 21-20 loss to Daingerfield in the area round of the 2002 Class 3A playoffs.

The longest winning streak in the state's largest classification in the last fifty years was Southlake Carroll's thir-

The field house at Abilene High was named in honor of Chuck Moser in 1988. This is the plaque that was dedicated in Moser's honor. (Photo courtesy of Abilene High museum)

ty-one-game win streak in 2002-03 that was finally snapped by Katy in the 2003 Class 5A Division II title game. But Southlake Carroll's streak was eighteen games short of Abilene's incredible winning skein.

The Texas Sports Writers Association named Moser the state's Coach of the Year in 1956 and 1957. Only six teams—Breckenridge, Sweetwater, San Angelo, Odessa, Pampa, and Wichita Falls (twice)— were able to beat Moser's Eagles in his seven seasons in Abilene. Highland Park and Sweetwater each managed a tie. He coached fifteen first-team all-staters in his seven years in Abilene.

IMPACT ON PLAYERS

Moser's legacy, however, goes much deeper than just victories, donuts, rose bushes, and all-state selections. He left a lasting impact on the players who played for him.

"Moser was just what the Eagles needed," long-time *Houston Chronicle* sports writer Bill McMurray wrote in his book, *Texas High School Football.* "He was at the right place at the right time, an opportunist with tremendous motivational talents, unquestioned football wisdom, and the organizational ability to fit all the pieces of the puzzle together. He blended the boys from the ranches with the boys from downtown Abilene into champions. They had poise, confidence and pride. They were the rage of the fifties, a howling wind from out of the west that left a lasting impact on Texas high school football."

Moser announced his retirement from coaching on January 15, 1960, to become the athletic director for the Abilene ISD, a job he would hold for the next fourteen years.

"Part of my job would be to help select the coaching staff and buy equipment for the new school (Cooper, which opened that fall)," he said, "and it wouldn't be fair for me to do so while still serving as head coach at Abilene High."

Years later, however, Moser admitted that a fear of losing may have also played a role in his early departure from the coaching profession.

"I was probably scared of getting beat," Moser said. "Really. We'd been winning. That year we invited the kids up from the junior high, our talent wasn't as good as what it had been. And we were dividing into two high schools. I knew we were going to get beat, and I didn't want to get beat. I guess that is being honest about it."

It took Abilene High forty more years to return to the playoffs and forty-two years to finally win a district championship after Moser claimed his sixth straight district crown in 1959.

An often-heard phrase when his former players talk about their coach is that Moser "was ahead of his time."

Many of Chuck Moser's former players at Abilene High joined Chuck and Doris Moser at the Cotton Bowl in 1986 when Moser and the other new members of the Texas Sports Hall of Fame were honored. (Photo courtesy of Doris Moser collection at Abilene High museum)

Wally Bullington, his former assistant and eventual successor, said Moser's off-season conditioning program helped develop the Abilene program. "He wanted them to do well in other sports. Gregory, Carpenter and Ash all played three sports. But he didn't want you sitting around in another sport. That's why he came up with an off-season program that was way ahead of its time. It helped kids to get faster and stronger.

"He went out and got drill bits from pipe companies, so we had weights. He was big on climbing ropes. He wanted you to go up a rope without using your legs. We were never very big. We worked on speed and quickness."

His eligibility slips were the forerunner of today's no-pass, no-play rule and emphasized the importance of academics.

Moser's teams were always incredibly well prepared. Many former players say Moser's scouting reports were far more sophisticated than what they experienced in college. Moser had his team ready

The 1986 inductees into the Texas Sports Hall of Fame (from left to right) were Forrest Gregg, Odus Mitchell, Elvin Hayes, Ernie Koy, Field Scovell, George Foreman, Chuck Moser and Carroll Shelby. (Photo courtesy of Doris Moser collection at Abilene High museum)

to play against ten different defenses, not just the defense their next opponent would be playing.

"When we were winning so many games, a lot of times a team might play a 5-2 defense," he said. "But when we came to play them, they'd change their defense entirely. So I had ten defenses that Bob Groseclose taught these kids, the third teamers and JV kids, how to play. After a week of practice, he and Blacky would take those kids and every play they would be in a different defense. It's a pretty good test for your players on offense. We never wanted to be surprised. Football is just like war. Everything is anticipation. If they throw, you knew they're going to throw the ball.

"Great football players anticipate. I had some great small linebackers. Sam Caudle had his two teeth knocked out all the time. When they came out of the huddle, Sam knew where the ball was going. I don't know how he did it. But small guys can play sometime if they're really smart."

STATISTICS BOOK

Moser also invented a way to keep statistics during the game that would allow him to make quick adjustments at halftime.

"John Dyer, a history teacher at Abilene High, kept the 'Quarterback Statistics Book' on the sideline at games," Bullington said. "It was a book that Moser invented. Beginning in 1962, Moser sold the book at coaching school. He could take the book at halftime and get a bird's-eye view of the game. You could get a performance picture of the game, play by play. He could look at it and say number seventy-two is making seventy percent of the tackles. And he could tell what play was working. He was the best coach in a game at making adjustment that I've ever known. Gordon Wood was a close second. That book was as modern as tomorrow. I'd never seen anything like it before, but I used it. I used it at ACU, too. He put it out (in 1962) to help kids and help coaches. He took what he knew and helped coaches."

Moser coached the North team to a 28-0 victory in the 1957 Coaching School all-star game and served as president of the Texas High School Coaches' Association in 1962-63.

In 1963, he was selected as an inductee in the inaugural class of the National High School Hall of Honor. Moser is also a member of the Texas High School Football Hall of Fame, the Texas Sports Hall of Fame, and the Big Country Athletic Hall of Fame.

Moser's successful blend of discipline, game preparation, emphasis on academics, and—of course—winning made the Eagles incredibly popular in a community that loved its high school football.

"I'd go to work on the day of the game, and there would be people who had slept out there all night at Eagle Gym to get tickets to the game that night," Bullington said. "Old Fair Park seated about 10,500, and we had half of that sold in season tickets. Our booster club meetings were held at the Coca Cola Auditorium on North First, and it was

FOOTBALL STATISTICS BOOK

FOR

QUARTERBACKS

COPYRIGHT 1961

BY

Chuck Moser

BOX 981   ABILENE, TEXAS 79604

$2.00

Chuck Moser invented a way to keep statistics during the game that would allow him to make quick adjustments at halftime. He sold his Quarterback Statistics Book at coaching clinics and athletic stores.

hard to get a seat. The booster club chartered trains to Odessa and other games."

"We had a lot of support," Moser recalled. "Everything was centered on one school. I know you have to have two schools, but it sure is fun to have just one."

Even *Sports Illustrated* came to Abilene to do a feature on Moser's amazing Eagles. They asked about the rumors that Abilene was recruiting players.

"We don't import players or move families," Moser told writer Don Parker. "But we do have a football program that beats almost anything you might find outside of Texas. We have over 800 kids playing football in eighteen elementary schools scattered around town. They all come to Abilene High. You win a lot and people get the idea that the kids on your team are supermen or over-age ringers. Look, the team's average age is 16.9 years, the average weight is 180. The reason these kids are good is that they want to be good. They work at it and they work hard."

Moser has had a life-long influence on the players that played for him.

Moser could look at the statistics book at halftime and get a bird's eye view of the game.

"My goodness, did he ever," said John Paul Young, a starting guard on the 1957 team. "I was from the wrong side of the tracks growing up, and he and the coaches took us in."

What made Moser so special?

"I don't know," Young said. "I think it was his character, his work ethic, his knowledge, and the way he handled people. He ran a very strict, rigid program. To be honest, I was scared to death of him. When he joined our staff at Texas A&M, someone asked me what I was going to call him. I said, 'It sure won't be Chuck.'"

Young's career as a coach is intertwined with Moser's. Young went to Texas Western, now known as Texas-El Paso, to play football after his high school career because "that's where Coach told me to go." It's a decision that he has never regretted. "I had wonderful years there and wonderful honors," he said. "I came out with a wonderful

The statistics book would tell Moser what plays were working and other details.

wife and children and grandchildren. I probably would have gone to Texas Tech, but I probably couldn't have played at other places, and Coach Moser knew that."

Young also met Bum Phillips during his stay at UTEP, an association that influenced Young's life almost as much as playing for Moser. Phillips was a young coach then on the Miners' staff.

"I was walking down the hall one day after my senior year," Young said, "and Bum handed me a list of things to do. I said, 'OK, Coach, I'll get on these this afternoon.' Bum said, 'No, you'll get on them right away. You work for me now.'"

Young was a graduate assistant coach under Phillips for one year at UTEP before taking a high school coaching job at Jacksonville, in East Texas, as an assistant for one of Phillips' best friends. He then coached at SMU and Oklahoma State before joining Gene Stallings' staff at Texas A&M. He stayed at A&M to coach under Emory Bellard

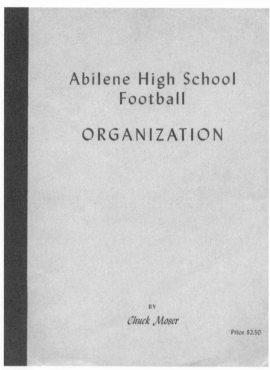

Abilene High School
Football

ORGANIZATION

BY
Chuck Moser

Price $2.50

Chuck Moser and assistant coach Wally Bullington compiled a book called "Abilene High School Football Organization" that was sold at coaching clinics. It includes all facets of Moser's program, including his philosophy, drills and rules.

when Stallings left to join the Dallas Cowboys. Bellard, who had coached against Moser at Breckenridge and later coached San Angelo to a state championship, asked Young one day in 1974 if he thought Moser would come work for him at Texas A&M.

"He's the athletic director in Abilene," Young told Bellard. "I don't think so, but I'll ask." He called Doris Moser and found out her husband would be interested in coaching at Texas A&M.

Moser had already announced his retirement as athletic director for the Abilene Independent School District, and a retirement party was planned at the AISD Administration Building. Young came to the event. With the help of Mrs. Moser and Shorty Lawson, Moser's successor as athletic director, they arranged for the phone to ring in the middle of the reception.

"Everybody knew about it except Chuck," Young said. It was Bellard calling on the phone, offering Moser a job on his staff at Texas A&M.

"I asked Emory how long I had to think about it, and he said take as long as you want," Moser recalled years later. "I called him back in ten minutes. I coached the backs one year. I coached the wide receivers and I coached on defense one year. Then they made the rule that you couldn't have more than nine coaches. We had nine, so I asked Emory if I could be the administrative assistant. I did that one year. Then I was the recruiting coordinator the last year. When you get older, it's hard to keep up with those younger guys, recruiting-wise."

"A few years later, Coach Moser was getting ready to retire at A&M," said Young, who was by then coaching on Phillips' staff with the Houston Oilers. "Bum said, "Do you think Chuck Moser would scout for us?' I said, 'I'll ask.' "

Again through the help of Doris Moser, Young arranged for a telephone call to interrupt Moser's retirement party at Texas A&M. This time, it was Phillips on the phone, offering Moser a scouting job with the Oilers.

Moser, who lived in Bryan-College Station after leaving Abilene until his death in 1995, continued to scout for the Oilers until Phillips left Houston for the New Orleans Saints. Then, on Phillips' recommendation, he landed a scouting job for the Canadian Football League before finally retiring for good a few years before his death.

PLAYER TESTIMONIALS

All of the players interviewed for this book talked about the profound influence that Moser, Hank Watkins, Bullington, and the other Abilene coaches had on their lives, but the most interesting comments are ones made more than forty-five years ago.

During the 1958 season, sports writer Don Oliver asked six former Abilene High players who were playing college football—Twyman Ash at Rice, Sammy Caudle at SMU, Bobby Jack Oliver and Jimmy Millerman at Baylor, David Bourland at Texas Tech, and H.P. Hawkins at Abilene Christian College—to write down their thoughts about Moser.

These were nineteen- and twenty-year-old college students giving public testimony to the impact that Moser had on their lives. Here are excerpts from those comments:

Bobby Jack Oliver: "Coach Moser has meant more to me than any coach I have ever had—not only as a coach but as a man. He is the type coach every football player dreams of playing under.

"On the practice field, not only did we work hard, but we enjoyed it. He was so enthusiastic that he would get right in the middle of a scrimmage, and I can remember more than once when he got his foot stepped on or got blocked, but he would always be laughing and ready to go.

"That smile and laugh is what really gets you. When we did something good or bad, he was the first one to tell us about it in a way that it would make us want to work just that much harder.

"He had so much confidence in us that it made us have confidence in ourselves. When we went out on the field we all felt that we couldn't be beat and if we did get beat (which was only twice) the next week we felt the same way.

"One of the things that I will never forget is right before we went out on the field for the first game under Coach Moser, everyone noticed that we hadn't had a pre-game prayer. One of the boys asked him if we could have one and he said, 'I say my prayers every night of the week before the game and I expect all of you to do the same.

"I just can't put my finger on where his greatness comes from, but I can tell you from my own personal experience, we all worship him and would do anything in the world for him."

Twyman Ash: "Playing under him has meant more to me than I could ever put in a short letter. It not only meant playing under and being associated with a great coach, but also being associated with a fine Christian man. At different times during my senior year in high school, I would watch him and just hope I could pattern my life after him.

"If it had not been for the background and guidance that Coach Moser gave me, I probably would never have obtained an athletic scholarship and a chance for a college education.

"He has given a number of boys the same guidance. I would never be able to repay him for all that he has done for me. Under him I learned the meaning of victory, defeat, humility, hard work, respect, sacrifice, and many others.

"He not only taught the boys football, but he taught them to look to the future. He was interested in each boy's grades, how they got along with their teachers and classmates, and also in their everyday activities. He helps each boy realize what an education would mean in the future. In his own words, 'You can't eat that football when you get out of school and have to make a living.'

"He checked the grades of each boy on report card day and for every point that you dropped in a subject you had to do extra running. I know from experience that those grades improved from time to time.

"I know that every boy that has played for Coach Moser has nothing but the highest respect for him in every way. Last year on the freshman football squad here at Rice, I played with two boys that played under Coach Moser their sophomore year at McAllen. They said that every boy and everyone in McAllen felt the same way about him as the people in Abilene do, and that they would have done anything to keep from losing him.

"While playing for him, I remember many incidents that hold pleasant memories for me. When he first came to Abilene, I was a sophomore and he requested that all the boys drop by his office and get acquainted. When I walked into his office and shook his hand, I was immediately scared to death of him. But, being the kind of man and coach that he is, it didn't take him long to erase my fears. Before long, I felt just as relaxed around him as I did my own dad.

"Playing on one of Coach Moser's teams is really an honor. His teams have a certain feeling among the boys that not other teams seem to have—you are all just like one big family."

Sam Caudle: "Playing for Coach Moser has probably been the luckiest thing that ever happened to me. He was interested not only in your athletics, but also in how you did in school, and I don't know if this is true of all coaches.

"I remember how we used to have to carry eligibility sheets around to the teachers each week and how we all hated them. We didn't dislike them just because of the inconvenience, but we knew if the teachers put anything bad on them it mean a little extra running after practice. It made better students out of us though, which is really paying off now. It's hard enough as it is, and I would hate to think where I'd be if I hadn't studied in high school

"Playing for Coach Moser has also been a great advantage to me as a football player. I didn't realize how much more we know about fundamentals and every other phase of the game until I played with boys who have all the ability in the world but don't do so good because they haven't had good coaching.

"Every boy who has played for Coach Moser is lucky to have had such good high school coaching. There are other boys who know just as much as we do about fundamentals, but you can tell that the big majority of them haven't been coached as well."

David Bourland: "I have never known a man as great as Coach Moser. While playing under Coach Moser, I learned much more than I could have ever learned by not being associated with him. I am not only talking about learning football, but just learning how to be a man of respect in everyday life.

"If we ever lost a game, Coach would never blame us. He always said, 'I should have worked harder.' Whenever one fellow takes the blame of forty others on his shoulders, one just can't help but like him.

"Now that I'm in college I can see why Coach did certain things he did while I was playing under him. I am very thankful to have been so lucky to play under Coach Moser. I am just sorry I couldn't be under him longer than I was."

Jimmy Millerman: "Coach Moser taught me a lot of things besides football. One thing he taught me was to have confidence in myself. Another thing that I consider important is that I learned not to worry about things.

"He always said that instead of worrying, you should think your problem out. I think these things have helped me a lot since I've gotten out of high school."

H.P. Hawkins: "I will certainly be one of the first to say that Mr. Chuck Moser is an outstanding coach. I will also agree that he is an outstanding gentleman and a builder of men.

"Training rules, such as no smoking and no drinking, are rules that most coaches have for their players in order to have a well-conditioned team. Coach Moser's teams have the same rules for the purpose of conditioning, but he also hopes the rules will stick with the players after their football days are over.

"After playing for Coach Moser, I know that there is no one who enjoys winning football games any more than he does. He is not the type of many, however, that will try to win a game at the expense of an injured player. He showed that during the 1954 state championship game against Stephen F. Austin of Houston. That was the first time one of his teams had reached the state finals, and he naturally wanted to win the game a little more than previous ones.

"He could have urged our usual starting offensive tackle, who had been injured earlier in the season, but he refused to play the boy for fear that the tackle might receive a permanent injury. This incident made me realize that Coach Moser was more concerned with the welfare of a player than winning a football game.

"Coach Moser wants more than good football players. He wants gentlemen who know how to act no matter where they are. He will not tolerate fighting or cursing and demands clean play at all times. These things are not taught by some coaches, and I feel that the boys playing under coaches not teaching these things are missing something.

"Having played for Coach Moser is something that I will always be proud of. He is the type of person and coach that any father should want his son to be associated with, whether it be as a football player, a Boy Scout, or as a student who knows him and has a chance to observe the fine example he sets."

MORE THAN WINNING

Former *Abilene Reporter-News* editor Dick Tarpley knew Moser well and kept up with him even after he left Abilene.

"Moser brought much more than winning to Abilene," Tarpley said. "*Time* magazine asked its regional correspondent to do a story about Moser's record, emphasizing the win-at-all-costs philosophy it believed to be inherent in Texas high schools. When the writer responded that Moser stressed academics, class attendance, and citizenship, *Time* decided the story lacked reader interest.

"Moser set the example for his players. He was president of the Abilene Kiwanis Club, headed his division of the United Way, was president of the Boy Scout Council, and chairman of the board at his church. He taught a junior high boys Sunday School class, even when the Eagles played on Saturday."

Moser is still remembered in many other ways in Abilene today. The building that houses the football locker rooms, weight room and offices at Abilene High is the "Chuck Moser Field House."

The Abilene Rotary Club, through the Abilene Community Foundation, manages the Chuck and Doris Moser Scholarship program, awarding college scholarships each year to deserving student athletes. A "Team of the Century" golf tournament raises money annually for another Chuck and Doris Moser Scholarship Fund for students attending Texas State Technical College. Many of the stars of the Abilene teams in the 1950s return each year to participate in the golf tournament.

For the last five years, the Rotary Club has also presented the Moser Coach of the Year Award to the top male and female coaches in the Big Country.

So what made the Abilene High football teams of the 1950s so good that today—even fifty years later—they are still considered the best in Texas history?

"Chuck Moser," Caudle said simply. "We were just kids, no different than anyone else."

Maybe Bill Sides, the all-state fullback on the 1957 squad, put it best. "Coach Moser was the right coach at the right place at the right time. We had a bunch of good players and a few great ones. The magic of what Chuck Moser did was to mold it all together."

He molded together a team, a coaching staff, a school, and a community—and the Abilene High Eagles became the Team of the Century, the greatest high school football team in Texas.

Team of the Century

Here is the list of the players, managers, and coaches who were members of the Abilene High School football teams (1953-59) under Chuck Moser, as pictured in *The Flashlight*, Abilene High School yearbook. The Moser squads were chosen the "Team of the Century" by the sports writers of the *Dallas Morning News* in 1999.

Butch Adams
Louis Adams
Ronnie Alldredge
Freddy Allen
Jack Anthony
Gaylord Armstrong
Ralph Arrell
Twyman Ash
Bobby Austin
Jerry Avery
Frank Aycock
Phil Bailey
Eddie Baldwin
John Barfoot
David Barrera
Don Beall
Bob Beck
Glen Belew
Ervin Bishop
Don Black
B.L. "Blacky" Blackburn
James Blackwood
Pat Bland
Charles Bradshaw
Robert Boatler
Charles Bottoms
David Bourland

Dan Boyd
Tommy Boyd
Charlie Bradshaw
Don Bridges
Truman Bridges
Jim Briggs
Harold Brinson
James Brooke
Ralph Bruton
Mike Bryant
Jim Buchanan
T.A. Buchanan
Wally Bullington
Rusty Burnett
Jim Busby
Ned Butler
Spider Bynum
Jim Carpenter
Bufford Carr
Sam Caudle
Ronnie Cearley
Neal Cloud
Carl Collum
Chuck Colvin
Gene Colvin
Henry Colwell
Ronnie Conklin

Maurice Cook
Larry Cooper
Stanley Cozby
Bobby Crawford
Reggie Crosby
Jack Crumpler
Rick Crumpler
Willis Ray Crumpler
Elmo Cure
Max Darden
Reyes T. Diaz
Jerry Paul Dillinger
Frank Etter
Chuck Evans
Charles Flynn
Ray Fraser
Bill Fuller
Dub Galbraith
Gervis Galbraith
Gerald Galbraith
Johnny Garner
Bob Gay
Jim Gilstrap
Nat Gleaton
Dale Graham
Chuck Green
Freddie Green

Glynn Gregory
Glen Griffin
Bob Groseclose
Ted Hamilton
Don Harber
Charles Harrison
Jack Harrison
H.P. Hawkins
Caleb Herndon
Charles Hilburn
Graham Holland
Joe Howard
Johnny Howe
David Howle
Bob Hubbard
Kenny Huffman
David Hughes
Don Hughes
Harold Hundley
Cullen Hunt
Ronnie Ingle
Jerry Jackson
Jimmy Johns
Leroy Johnston
Hubert Jordan
Rodney Joy
Leldon Kelso
Teddy Jack Key
Boyd King
Rufus King
Charles Lacy
William D. "Shorty" Lawson
Elwood Leonard

James Leonard
Frank Liles
Melvin Lindsey
Ted Lucas
Ronnie Luckie
Freddie Martinez
Tony Martinez
Charles McCook
Larry McCraw
Ronnie McDearman
Vance McFadden
Hal McGlothin
Mike McKinnis
Robert McKissick
Richard McPherson
Jim Millerman
Billy Monk
Weldon Moore
Tommy Morris
Clint Murphy
Butch Newman
Sarge Newman
Wylie Newman
Steve Newton
George Nichols
Bobby Jack Oliver
Noel Orr
Dick Orsini
Jerry Osborn
Nick Palmer
David Parks
Alan Peake
Stuart Peake
Mike Pelfry

Bill Perry
Jimmy Perry
Wendell Phillips
Henry Pinkston
Clevie Powell
Arch Ratliff
Jack Reese
Bennie Reid
Roy Reid
Don Rhoden
Larry Rhodes
Mike Richardson
Denny Roberts
Jim Roberts
Clark Robinson
Jim Rose
Homer Rosenbaum
Billy Jack Rudd
Johnny Russell
Jon Sandefer
Frank Scarbrough
Bob Schick
Kenny Schmidt
Rex Scott
Jack Self
Bill Sides
James Smith
Don Smothers
Andy Springer
Mac Starnes
Charles Steinman
David Steinman
Charles Steph
Harold Stephens

Carlton Stowers

Steve Strickland

Bob Swafford

Hollis Swafford

Jim Tatum

Joe Taylor

Bill Teague

John Thomas

Rip Thomas

Paul Tidwell

Les Townsend

Jimmy Tutt

Joe Vick

Bill Walker

Tim Walter

Joe Ward

H.D. "Hank" Watkins

Mike Wayman

James Welch

Guy Wells

Charles Williams

Gerald Williamson

David Winkles

Kim Winston

Eddie Woods

Glenn Woods

Jim Yarborough

Tommy Yarbro

John Paul Young

Bob Youngblood

The scores from the Moser years

1953 7-2-1
28-13 Dallas Highland Park
13-13 Sweetwater
19-6 Breckenridge
60-0 Borger
14-19 Odessa
6-7 Pampa
32-7 Amarillo
28-0 Lubbock
39-13 Midland
61-0 San Angelo

1954 12-1
40-0 Dallas Highland Park
13-0 Sweetwater
13-35 Breckenridge
34-7 Borger
21-7 Odessa
41-7 Pampa
47-0 Amarillo
35-7 Lubbock
28-14 Midland
27-0 San Angelo
61-0 El Paso Austin
(bi-district)
46-0 Fort Worth Poly
(semifinals)
14-7 Houston Austin
(state championship)

1955 13-0
34-0 Dallas Highland Park
45-20 Sweetwater
13-0 Breckenridge
35-6 Borger
47-0 Odessa
40-12 Pampa
35-13 Amarillo
62-7 Lubbock
28-7 Midland
35-6 San Angelo
61-0 El Paso (bi-district)
33-6 Dallas Sunset
(semifinals)
33-13 Tyler
(state championship)

1956 14-0
41-6 San Antonio Edison
39-7 Sweetwater
41-0 Lubbock Monterey
41-0 Breckenridge
49-7 Lubbock
45-14 Waco
42-6 Big Spring
47-6 Odessa
41-6 Midland
20-0 San Angelo
42-6 El Paso Ysleta
(bi-district)
14-0 Fort Worth Paschal
(quarterfinals)
20-6 Wichita Falls
(semifinals)
14-0 Corpus Christi Ray
(state championship)

1957 12-0-1

26-13 San Antonio Jefferson
34-13 Sweetwater
58-0 Lubbock Monterey
41-20 Breckenridge
39-0 Lubbock
27-7 Waco
32-0 Big Spring
19-0 Odessa
41-0 Midland
12-6 San Angelo
60-0 El Paso Austin
      (bi-district)
33-14 Amarillo
      (quarterfinals)
20-20 Dallas Highland Park
      (semifinals)

1958 10-2

28-26 San Antonio Jefferson
0-19 Sweetwater
34-0 Lubbock Monterey
22-0 Breckenridge
52-8 Austin Travis
36-0 Waco
38-8 Big Spring
34-14 Odessa
29-6 Midland
12-0 San Angelo
40-6 El Paso Ysleta (bi-district)
6-34 Wichita Falls
      (quarterfinals)

1959 10-2

14-12 San Antonio Jefferson
29-12 Sweetwater
14-13 Breckenridge
42-0 San Antonio Alamo Heights
13-12 Waco
36-0 Big Spring
44-0 Odessa Permian
7-0   Odessa
28-7 Midland
0-13 San Angelo
45-0 El Paso Ysleta
      (bi-district)
12-26 Wichita Falls
      (quarterfinals)

Starting Lineups

Here are the starting lineups for Chuck Moser's seven teams at Abilene High as compiled by former *Abilene Reporter-News* editor Dick Tarpley. In some cases, players split time at certain position, and in those cases both players are listed as starters:

1953
OFFENSE
Ends – Twyman Ash, Bob Gay
Tackles – Bobby Jack Oliver, Dan Boyd
Guards – Dick Orsini, Frank Liles
Center – Mac Starnes
Quarterback – Don Harber
Halfbacks – Jimmy Millerman, Wendell Phillips
Fullback – Ronnie McDearman

DEFENSE
Defensive ends – Bob Gay, Ray Fraser
Defensive linemen – Bobby Jack Oliver, John Thomas, Frank Liles
Linebackers – Mac Starnes, Dick Orisini, Bill Perry
Cornerbacks – Twyman Ash, Larry McCraw
Defensive halfbacks – Don Rhoden, Jimmy Millerman

1954
OFFENSE
Ends – Twyman Ash, Hollis Swafford
Tackles – Cullen Hunt, Glenn Woods
Guards – John Thomas, Sam Caudle
Center – Elmo Cure
Quarterback – H.P. Hawkins
Halfbacks – Jimmy Millerman, Henry Colwell
Fullback – Jim Briggs

DEFENSE

Defensive ends – Bob Hubbard, Stuart Peake

Defensive linemen – John Thomas, Cullen Hunt, Rufus King, Glenn Woods, Weldon Moore

Linebackers – Sam Caudle, David Steinman

Cornerbacks – Twyman Ash, Henry Colwell

Defensive halfbacks – David Bourland, Jimmy Millerman

1955

OFFENSE

Ends – Freddie Green, Jerry Avery

Tackles – Rufus King, Homer Rosenbaum

Guards – Stuart Peake, Sam Caudle

Center – Elmo Cure

Quarterback – David Bourland

Halfbacks – Glynn Gregory, Henry Colwell

Fullback – James Welch

DEFENSE

Defensive ends – Guy Wells, Stuart Peake

Defensive linemen – Rufus King, Bufford Carr, Elmo Cure

Linebackers – Sam Caudle, James Welch

Cornerbacks – Freddie Green, Henry Colwell

Defensive halfbacks – Glynn Gregory, Jimmy Carpenter, David Bourland

1956

OFFENSE

Ends – Rufus King, Kenny Schmidt

Tackles – Boyd King, Clint Murphy, Bufford Carr

Guards – Stuart Peake, Guy Wells, Hubert Jordan

Center – Jim Rose

Quarterback – Harold Stephens, Gervis Galbraith

Halfbacks – Glynn Gregory, Jimmy Carpenter

Fullback – Bill Sides, Charles Bradshaw

DEFENSE
Defensive ends – Stuart Peake, Guy Wells, Ervin Bishop
Defensive linemen – Rufus King, Bufford Carr
Linebackers – Jim Rose, Gerald Galbraith, Hubert Jordan
Cornerbacks – Charles Bradshaw, Gervis Galbraith
Defensive halfbacks – Glynn Gregory, Jimmy Carpenter

1957
OFFENSE
Ends – Jimmy Perry, Mike McKinnis
Tackles – Mike Bryant, Ronnie Alldredge
Guards – John Young, Truman Bridges
Center – Gerald Galbraith, Alan Peake
Quarterback – Gervis Galbraith
Halfbacks – Stanley Cozby, Chuck Colvin
Fullback – Bill Sides

DEFENSE
Defensive ends – Ronnie Ingle, Dale Graham, Don Hughes
Defensive linemen – Mike Bryant, Frank Aycock, John Young
Linebackers – Truman Bridges, Gerald Galbraith, Bill Sides
Cornerbacks – Gervis Galbraith, Charles Harrison
Halfbacks – Jimmy Perry, Bob Swafford

1958
OFFENSE
Ends – David Parks, Louis Adams
Tackles – Frank Aycock, Jerry Osborn
Guards – Rip Thomas, Don Hughes
Center – Arch Ratliff
Quarterback – Freddie Martinez
Halfbacks – Stanley Cozby, Tim Walter, Sarge Newman, Andy Springer
Fullback – Charles Harrison

DEFENSE

Defensive ends – Jerry Osborn, Don Hughes

Defensive linemen – Frank Aycock, Jimmy Gilstrap, Leroy Johnston

Linebackers – Charles Harrison, Ray Crumpler

Cornerbacks – David Parks, Reggie Crosby

Defensive halfbacks – Charles Lacy, Charles McCook,
        Andy Springer

1959

OFFENSE

Ends – David Parks, Clevie Powell, Louis Adams

Tackles – Jimmy Gilstrap, Ralph Arrell, Bill Walker

Guards – Rip Thomas, J.W. Howard, Leroy Johnston, Ray Crumpler,
        Neal Cloud

Center – Arch Ratliff

Quarterback – Charles McCook

Halfbacks – Sarge Newman, T.A. Buchanan, Bobby Austin,
        Gerald Williamson

Fullback – Wylie Newman, Mike Wayman, Ray Crumpler

DEFENSE

Defensive ends – Leroy Johnston, Bobby Schick, Louis Adams

Defensive linemen – Jimmy Gilstrap, Rip Thomas, Ray Crumpler,
        Tommy Boyd, Bill Walker

Linebackers – Ray Crumpler, Joe Howard, Paul Tidwell,
        Wylie Newman

Cornerbacks – David Parks, T.A. Buchanan, Dub Galbraith,
        Jack Harrison

Defensive halfbacks – David Winkles, Sarge Newman,
        Gerald Williamson

EXCERPTS

from Chuck Moser's *Abilene High School Football Organization*

CAPTAIN'S CHECK LIST
1. 5 time outs.
2. Save time outs for last of 2nd and 4th quarters.
3. Get team together at time outs (do not sit down).
4. Do not permit talking in huddle.
5. Need captain when things are going wrong or behind.
6. Don't criticize - Encourage the good.
7. On all decisions time is out.
    Take your time, time is out.
    Think
    In case of doubt call on defensive or offensive quarterback.
8. Watch all measurements.
9. If you need a player, come and tell me what position you need.
10. Check with me always just before the flip.

RULES EVERYONE SHOULD KNOW
1. The ball is never dead until the referee's whistle kills it. (Play til you hear the whistle.)
2. The horn or gun doesn't stop the play. (Always finish the play.)
3. Fair catch—When the safety signals with his arm over his head. (He can't run, don't hit him—it is 15 yards)
4. Do not interfere with a man catching a punted ball unless it is rolling toward you, cover it however. Never touch a punted ball inside the 10 yard line, it is a touchback.
5. After a safety the ball is put in play by a kick-off from the 20 yard line.
6. A field goal should be played just like a punted ball. You can block it and run with it.
7. We must always have 7 men within one foot of the ball on offense.

8. You can block the passer after he throws the ball, but you can't tackle him.

9. Do not touch the punter unless you can block the kick.

10. Only ends and backs are eligible to receive a forward pass. Quarterbacks, guards, and tackles cannot go over 1 yd. past the line of scrimmage til the pass is thrown; any one is eligible for a lateral pass.

11. A lateral pass is a free ball, any offensive player can run with it, defensive players can intercept a lateral, and run.

12. Substitution:

a. There are 5 time outs per half.

b. Any substitution made while the clock is running and before the referee leaves the ball, costs one time out, but we don't get it. The clock starts when the ball is snapped.

c. If a substitution is made after 5 time outs or after the referee leaves the ball, it costs 5 yds. and the clock starts when the referee leaves the ball.

d. When the ball changes hands, after a kick-off or any time out we can sub as many as 11 players.

e. Any player who leaves the field must remain out at least one play.

13. Defensive holding is when you are not trying to get to the ball carrier.

14. A back cannot crawl with the ball, and no teammate can shove or push him.

15. When you block on offense you must have your arm in contact with your jersey; this is not true on a side body block.

16. Clipping is blocking it the back.

17. You have 25 seconds between plays to put the ball in play.

18. A kick off is a free ball if it goes 10 yds. (It is a TD if you fall on it in the end zone.)

19. After the center adjusts the ball once, he cannot move it. No one can interlock their legs except the center and guards.

20. No offensive player can make a false start or head bob to draw the offense off sides.

21. It is unsportsman to cuss or when on defense to disconcert your opponent by counting or etc.
22. Incomplete pass—<u>Stops the clock</u>
   Time out called.
   Measurement for a first down
   Any kind of score.
   Penalty
   Ball goes out of bounds
23. You can intercept a pass in the end zone, the ball goes out to the 20 yd. line.
24. When the second kick off goes out of bounds, your opponents get the ball on the 50 yd. line. Not so if touched by the receiving team.
25. No back can be within one yd. of the line of scrimmage, unless he is on the line of scrimmage.
26. No lineman can be put in the backfield unless the captain tells the referee, except if he is over 5 yds. back (punter).
27. Any player who goes out of bounds is not eligible for a pass.
28. If any defensive player touches a forward pass, any offensive player can catch the ball and run.
29. A player will be suspended from the game for illegal use of the <u>knee</u>, <u>kicks</u>, <u>forearm</u>, <u>elbow</u>, <u>fist</u>, or <u>interlocked arms</u>.
30. Any player can run with a blocked punt that doesn't cross the line of scrimmage.
31. Any player can intercept a pass on defense.
32. You can't trip an opponent.

WHAT CAUSES MOST DEFEATS
   Intercepted passes (be ready to cover)
   Fumbles
   Blocked kicks
   Permitting long runs or passes

WHAT WINS GAMES
>The desire to win
>Downfield blocking
>Faking
>Maximum effort by every player on every play

SOMETHING TO READ AND THINK ABOUT

1. All great athletes are humble and do not show their emotions on the field. If you make a mistake, forget it and think about the next play. I think the boy who is mature emotionally will be able to endure pain with courage, wait for rewards, work for success, and take an active interest in the welfare of the total team—<u>not just himself</u>.

2. CONFIDENCE—Confidence is a mental state which, of course, is necessary for success in any phase of life. Confidence can be gained by experience. Some boys have difficulty understanding criticism and lose confidence when criticized. Others understand that severe constructive criticism often is a good sign of interest by the coach. The coach seldom wastes his breath if he is not interested in a boy.

3. VICTORY SPIRIT—To be a successful football player the boy must have a tremendous desire to win. He must be willing to work, wait, and sacrifice for victory.

4. LOYALTY—No football player will ever be great unless he has a certain amount of loyalty in his heart. The spirit of loyalty is more than giving all as far as physical effort goes. It involves a devotion to a cause. Always put your school and teammates ahead of yourself and you will be a loyal happy person.

5. RESPECT—The respect of a player for the fans, faculty, and teammates is invaluable.

6. POISE—Know that you know what to do on all occasions. Poise is developed by practice, learning, confidence, and experience.

7. RELIGION—The boy who has faith in God can look to the future without worry or strain. I firmly believe that the boys on

our team who attend church are more likely to be successful because they can face their problems with hope and encouragement. Religion plays an important part in the mental attitude of the athlete.

TRAINING RULES
1. No smoking or drinking.
2. Home at 10:00, except on Saturday and Friday—11:30.
3. Do not eat between meals.
4. Take care of all injuries (show coach always).
5. No dates the night before a ball game.

RULES IN THE DRESSING ROOM:
1. Read the bulletin board everyday.
2. Turn your equipment in each day.
3. No fighting or horse-play.
4. No cussing.
5. Stay out of the equipment room.
6. Save your energy for the field and act like a gentleman.
7. Do not wear shoes inside the dressing room.
8. Keep your equipment clean.
9. Always clean and polish your shoes the day before a game.

RULES ON THE FIE1D:
1. Be on time.
2. <u>Do not sit down</u>.
3. Run and hustle when you hear the whistle.
4. Do not cuss (keep your poise and don't lose your temper).
5. Do not leave the field (this means water).
6. Save conversation with spectators until after practice.
7. On the field, always be in full uniform, including helmet.

GENERAL RULES:
1. You must be enrolled in four subjects and passing three sub-jects in order to be eligible to play the next week.
2. Show your teachers and school the highest kind of respect.
3. Turn your eligibility slip in to coach's gym office by Thursday 8:30 A.M.
4. Make every practice a good one.
5. We need boys with the right spirit and hustle.
6. Do not go to the doctor without Coach Moser's permission.
7. Please don't steal from your school or teammates.
8. Do not miss practice without telling the coach first.

ASK YOURSELF EACH DAY BEFORE SUPPER,
"DID I IMPROVE TODAY?"
Take care of your body.—Dry good between your toes and hair after showering. Take good care of your feet.—Wear good, clean socks. Watch for signs of blisters. Be sure your shoes fit and are laced tight and high.

FOOD
Drink lots of milk. In hot weather drink as little as possible before eating.
Eat foods that give you energy as: eggs, meat, breakfast food, fruit, vegetables, potatoes (not fried), graham crackers and honey.
Do not eat between meals—malts, candy, and ice cream. OK right after a meal.
Stay away from pasteries, doughnuts, popcorn, nuts, fried food, and cokes.
These foods are not rules but only suggestions.

READ ONCE A WEEK
1. You must have confidence in your coaches, your teammates, and yourself in order to have a winning team.
2. The team that won't be beat, can't be beat.

3. Don't argue with the officials; treat them with respect and call them "sir."
4. Be a ball hawk; the team that recovers the most fumbles usually wins.
5. You will get blocked, but <u>never</u> <u>stay</u> <u>blocked</u>.
6. You won't score any touchdowns with the ball you just fumbled.
7. Remember you play the game on Friday just like you practiced all week.
8. You can't win the game with a million points if you let the other team get a million and one points.
9. When on defense, hope that they will throw the ball so we can intercept the ball.
10. There is no substitute for condition except the substitute sitting on the bench waiting for your job.
11. A winner never quits and a quitter never wins.
12. There is no system of football that does not depend on the hard and conscientious effort of every player on every play.
13. Don't lose your temper; no one wants it.
14. Good football players know the rules.
15. The <u>main</u> <u>thing</u> a boy wants to cultivate is the will to be the best.